CONFRONTING HISTORY AND HOLOCAUST
COLLECTED ESSAYS: 1972-1982

by

Jack Nusan Porter
Harvard University

Comprehensive Bibliography of Porter's Works

UNIVERSITY
PRESS OF
AMERICA

LANHAM • NEW YORK • LONDON

Dedicated to
Joseph Almuly
(1898-1982)

Jack Nusan Porter

TABLE OF CONTENTS

INTRODUCTION

This book is the second of four projected volumes of my collected essays. The first has already been published and deals with the issue of marginality and creativity (<u>The Jew as Outsider</u>, University Press of America, 1981). The third volume will cover the subject of neo-Nazism, neo-fascism, and cognate areas; while the fourth volume will deal with sociological theory: pure and applied.

This book, dear reader, that you hold in your hands is a collection of personal essays, a confrontation with history and holocaust. It is divided into three parts. The first part confronts my role as writer and outsider and covers in somewhat chronological order my evolution from high school (seen through the hindsight of a class reunion) to the making of a sociologist at the university to the death of my father. It ends with and then flows into the second half, a confrontation with the Holocaust. Here the essays are more scholarly but also quite personal; Jewish women in the resistance, Holocaust "therapy" for survivors and their children, Ukrainian-Jewish relations, neo-Nazis in the USA, and the affirmation of life after the Holocaust.

The book concludes with a chronological listing of all my writings (books, essays, articles, reviews) and speeches since 1967. I hope people will find it useful.

I could have rewritten some "dated" essays but I wanted to keep the fire and passion of the piece just as I wrote it. Times have changed and the prophetic vision has dimmed as I enter my middle years but oh, the memories of that flame. It wouldn't take much to rekindle it.

Some dozen-and-a-half books and 150 articles and reviews later (all under the age of 38), my friends are astounded at my productivity. So am I. I asked two other (more) prolific friends, Jacob Neusner and I.L. Horowitz, how they do it and the answer was simple: you must write <u>every</u> chance you get <u>regularly</u>: weekends, sick days, any day. Neusner does it everyday except Shabbat. Horowitz every weekend and holiday. In fact, aside from my family, I do little else but write. I socialize infrequently. I don't go to bars or movies. I engage in few sports. My compulsion, my

passion, and my relaxation is to write. I get very
<u>panicky</u> if I go more than a few months without writing.

Like all my books, I have a few people to thank:
Jerie Larsen, Dudley Glover, and the staff of Communication Graphics for their word-processing and support;
the Memorial Foundation for Jewish Culture for a grant
to study neo-Nazis; to my nephew, Mark Palmeri for sug-
gesting the title; to my wife Miriam and little son
Gabriel Alexander for their patience; and to Joseph
Almuly, my father-in-law, who passed away in the summer
of 1982, aged 84. I dedicate this book to him and to
his wife Reli and sister Lea.

Jack Nusan Porter
Ukrainian Research Institute
Harvard University
Chanukah, 1982

I. CONFRONTING HISTORY

NOTES OF AN INSIDER/OUTSIDER

My deep interest in Jewish life, religion, and politics evolved out of my family history. My parents' lives read like a novel by Leon Uris or Meyer Levin. My father was born in 1906 and my mother in 1910 in Volynia, Ukraine, Russia. They survived World War I, the Depression in Europe, and a thousand-and-one other travails, culminating in World War II and the Nazi horror. But their troubles were not over: next came DP camps in Austria, and escape from Europe. After the gates to Israel were closed to them -- America.

My father, Israel Puchtik (later Irving Porter) and my mother Faye Merin Porter, had been active in the Soviet anti-Nazi partisan movement from 1942-1944. They were members of the Kruk Fighting Group. These harrowing years left a deep impression on their three children -- my brother Solomon, a rabbi and rosh yeshiva, my sister, Bella, married to a rabbi and teacher, and me. There were two more children -- Chaya Udel and Pessel. They were machine-gunned in a field outside Manievich, Ukraine on September 23, 1942. They were only four and two years old.

When I asked my father why he had fought the Nazis, he answered very simply, "For revenge." It was his greatest concern that someone should survive to tell the world. He has a wartime diary (in Yiddish) that ought to be translated one day (by me?). So that his children should remember always, my father taught all of us to maintain a high level of religious responsibility and fervently commanded us never to forget what had happened during the Holocaust. My father has always been a model to me.

I did not personally experience the Holocaust, but this does not prevent me from joining those who have. I have become a witness. To remember the past is the path to self-realization. The past must be remembered not in order to suffer, but to liberate oneself and others toward the exhilaration of one's Judaism and the exaltation of life. The Jew, as fighter and writer, must remember and record. I have learned from my talks with Elie Wiesel and from his books and speeches. I have listened to other witnesses and have gathered their memoirs in a two-volume set, <u>Jewish Partisans: A Documentary of Jewish Resistance in the Soviet Union During World War II</u> (University Press of America, 1982) and in shorter articles published in magazines and newspapers during the past ten years.

After coming to the USA in 1946, we moved to Chicago and then to Milwaukee, a pleasant town and ironically peopled by Germans, Ukrainians, Poles, Lithuanians, and others who, at a different time and place, would be our enemies. I attended Hebrew and Sunday school; later the University of Wisconsin and Northwestern University where I received my Ph.D. in sociology in 1971. Since then I have taught at a variety of colleges in Chicago, New York, and Boston, but it was in graduate school at Northwestern University, that I changed the most. Coming from a gentle and conservative ghetto in Milwaukee, I was totally unprepared for the big-city radicalism of Chicago and the late 1960's. I found myself in a dilemma, "on the line" so to speak, caught between my religious upbringing and the modern world, between being a Jew and being an American; between being a Zionist and a socialist (a democratic socialist, of course, like Irving Howe, Michael Harrington, Eugene V. Debs, Golda Meir, and Helen Keller).

This tightrope that I walk between the particularism of my people and the universal concerns of the world does not always oscillate in ambivalence. If allowed to, it can lead to a creative tension that can produce cross-fertilizations among innovative ideas. I stand both within society and outside it, and this gives me an insight into both the internal and external side of my Self.

In my graduate school years at Northwestern University from 1967 to 1971, I struggled to maintain a balance between the particularism of my Jewish identity and the universalism of the intellectual/scholarly world. This struggle has marked my work from that period on, expressing itself best in my collected essays The Jew as Outsider (University Press of America, 1981). What I have gone through is not unique. There are many examples of Jewish intellectuals who have had to make peace with anti-Semitism, assimilation, and rejection by an often hostile, nervous and aloof Gentile society.

I have often found myself in the position of the "eternal middleman" -- too radical for some Jews; too Jewish for some radicals and liberals; too scholarly for popular magazines; too journalistic for academic journals; too rebellious to play ball with the cautious conformists; too pragmatic and wary for the radical true-believers. In short, the quintessential Jew -- questioning, probing, cautious, impulsive, and always alert. These are the traits of the survivor.

I was active in SDS and other radical groups when I felt they were right about Vietnam and racism. I left them when they turned violent and suicidal. (We called it "Custeristic" at the time.) I supported the Black Panther Party and other black militants when I felt they were being repressed by the police and the FBI, but when they turned anti-Zionist and anti-Semitic, I left them in the late 1960's to become one of the founders of the Jewish Student Movement. We, in the movement, were as turned off by the crazy radicals as we were by the pompous Jewish establishment. We had to find a golden mean, one both Jewish and progressive, Zionist and non-reactionary.

I feel a very deep kinship with two very different Jewish writers: the late Meyer Levin, and Karl Kraus, the great early 20th century Austrian satirist and writer. I understand Levin's battles with the literary and the Jewish world. He was a committed Zionist and Jew long before it was fashionable, and he was made to suffer greatly because of it. I resonate with Kraus' tempestuous assault on bourgeois -- in fact any "values" that lead to the corruption of civilization, especially through the defilement of language. In the words of Harry Zohn, Kraus was as passionate a lover as he was productive a hater. I wish I had more of his guts.

I turned to writing as a means of expressing the deep rage I felt in the 1960's. I expressed it best in a short essay I wrote for Writer's Digest in December 1974. Everything I put into that piece I felt deeply, but I am less angry today and somewhat more sensible. Like Jerry Rubin, I'm involved in raising a family and making money. The '60s seem far away, but I still try to read a bit of Karl Kraus whenever I need to get my dander up, and, believe me, that doesn't take much today. We're still facing the same problems we faced in the 1960s. Difficult however is trying to prove that making money is not antithetical to being a socialist.

How does a Jewishly-committed writer survive today? I wonder who reads my books and articles. Do they make any impact at all? I know that my anthology, with Peter Dreier, Jewish Radicalism (Grove Press, 1973) has achieved a kind of classic underground status and that outsider groups (feminists, gays, radicals, and others) still study it profitably nearly ten years later. But who else? Are students out there still interested? The established academics de-emphasize the impact of the Jewish countercultural/radical movement of the 1960s; even well-known Israeli scholars have never heard of it. Yet there are good people in the teaching profession who do not forget and we are re-introduced to new generations of Jewish students and scholars all the time.

When you write a great deal, some scholars think that you are a hack, superficial, or a dilettante. While one good book or article can make you famous forever, most great writers have written a great deal, and the good, sooner or later, triumphs over the bad.

There is still not enough respect given to the Jewish writer and scholar, and less for the lonely Hebrew or Yiddish teacher. Ten years ago in the Cats-kills, I was asked to give a talk on Jewish radicalism as a part of a panel with Carl Gershman. The keynote speaker that evening was Rabbi Abraham Joshua Heschel, one of the great Jewish theologians of this century. He was to receive the Anti-Defamation League's "Man of the Year" award that night. This prophetic-looking, frail man (he was not well and died soon after) arose and said: "You have given this award to President Kennedy, President Johnson, even Konrad Adenauer.... It is about time you gave it to a Hebrew teacher. I accept this award in behalf of all the unsung and unknown Hebrew teachers in the world". His chiding was gentle yet powerful, but he was soon forgotten amidst the jingling of stem-ware at the cocktail party that followed. While others joined in the revelry, a small group of us -- students, teachers, Heschel's daughter and wife, and a few nuns -- sat with Rabbi Heschel in a small alcove, discussing Torah. What those Jewish machers missed: we had Reb Heschel all to ourselves! I don't think they've given the award to a Hebrew teacher since.

Scholars are still respected, but who cares for the lowly Hebrew teacher? We have lost a great many fine teachers: Heschel, Paul Goodman, Abraham Maslow, and my old Hebrew teachers, Mssrs. Schwartzman, Pais, and Melrood. But for all that, there are many fine

Jewish-studies professors, Sunday and day-school teachers, and Talmud Torah instructors still quietly doing their work. Many students are turning to adult yeshivot; even some very famous writers and celebrities have discovered the Torah: Herman Wouk, Irving Wallace and his family, Barbra Streisand.

Despite the great sums spent on grand synagogues and community centers, on projects in Israel and for Soviet Jews, Jewish survival still depends upon these lowly Hebrew and Yiddish teachers.

This simple conclusion may seem incongruous coming from an ex-SDS leader and Jewish radical, but I am no longer a Jewish radical but a radical Jew! I am the son of Holocaust survivors and a survivor myself. I lost twenty-five members of my family to the Nazis, and despite all the ideologies and fads that abound, I am first a Jew. This is my rock. I owe this to my dead sisters and my dead uncles and aunts; and to my wife's family who perished during the war; to my father who died a few years ago and to my loving mother; and to my brother and sister. Most of all, I owe to my young son Gabriel that there will be a vibrant authentic Jewish civilization when he reaches my age.

Recently I have turned to an examination of faith and ethics, and the relationship between religion and political action. One may call it a search for moral action based on the prophetic vision of decency and good will; for equality and freedom however much these words (but not the concepts) have become overused and cliched. This vision perpetuates my parents' struggle to survive and their hope for a better world without death camps, terrorism and war. Theirs is the legacy that lives on in my writings and speeches. For this I thank them and bless them and trust that my writings are worthy of their sacrifices.

1982

THE JEWISH WRITER

I haven't been a writer for very long. But I've seen a lot, and there has been a lot to remember and a lot to forget, but I can't forget.

I've only started to write -- really write -- in the past few years. Before that, I wrote a million words of bullshit for teachers from kindergarten to graduate school. Most of it was "creative crap," written to please a teacher or pass a course. There were really only two times that I wrote what I wanted to write. The first was as an undergraduate at the University of Wisconsin in an English course taught by a grizzled old alcoholic English professor. My papers were all about my experiences in the banana field plantation of a kibbutz in the upper Galilee on a program of work/study in Israel in 1962 at the age of 17. He liked them because they were so real and filled with so much love -- love for the land, for the people, and especially for the old Arab workers who toiled along side us.

The second time was as a freelancer for an underground paper in Milwaukee -- The Daily Bugle. I wrote about growing up, my high school years -- about the jocks, the greasers, Elvis, the principal who committed suicide (carbon monoxide fumes), duck-tail haircuts, the grade-grubbing, the cheerleaders -- and I compared it all to my "homecoming" trip some ten years later. The school had changed, the students had changed, but the teachers hadn't. I didn't know it then but most of our teachers were white-collar racists. Neighborhood in transition. Blacks. Protests. Walk-outs. Broken windows. "You were the last of the great classes, Jack," a teacher moaned. I felt only pity. He died of a heart attack a month later. A victim of Black Power.

Getting a Ph.D. in sociology later was more of the same. Academic "training" nearly ruined my style. I was writing for a committee, not for myself. I finally broke away in a schizophrenic manner -- writing an academic dissertation at night for THEM; writing about protest and Jews and the past later in the night for ME.

When I began to write in earnest, I found that the words flowed, and people liked it. People like Kenneth Keniston and Elie Wiesel encouraged me to continue.

It started with two books -- one, completed and published by Grove Press, <u>Jewish Radicalism: A Selected Anthology</u>, co-edited with a friend of mine from the University of Chicago, Peter Dreier and, like myself, a former journalist turned sociologist turned journalist again; the other, a work in progress called <u>The Jewish Rebel: An Informal History of Jewish Radicalism from Moses to Marx to Marcuse</u>.*

These books plus my activity in the radical movement -- from SDS to the Jewish activist groups and a little flirtation along the way with the Jewish Defense League -- catapulted me into a search for identity, a search for roots, back towards to past.

The blacks were to blame. Hadn't they told us to get the hell out of their movement, to go among our own kind, to understand who <u>we</u> were...and then come back and talk?

The Isaeli-Arab 1967 Six-Day War was to blame. Hadn't that touched off fears of another holocaust? Hadn't that rekindled fantasies of the Maccabees, the partisans, the Stern Gang, Arie Ben-Canaan and the Irgun, Moshe Dayan, the Jews with "balls," the Jew with a gun in one hand and a Bible in the other?

The search for identity sent me scurrying to the psychiatrist's couch, the Institute of Ability (Zen and sensitivity), gestalt and encounter groups, astrology, acid, pot, Krishnamurti. Some turned to communes, some to Jesus: I turned back to my people -- Israel and the Holocaust.

* * * *

I knew I was different. Doubly or triply alienated. I was labeled a radical, most Americans are not. I was an immigrant from Russia, most Americans are not. I was a survivor, along with my parents; the rest of my family was lost to the unspeakable, the inscrutable -- the ovens of Auschwitz.

My father wasa partisan in the Russian underground for three years in the woods near Rovno, in the Ukraine, from 1942-1945. A simple yet profoundly wise man of the <u>shtetl</u>, he continues to counsel me: "Jack, follow ideas, not groups or leaders."

When I asked why he fought the Nazis, he answered with a very simple truth: "For revenge." His deepest concern was that somehow someone would survive to tell the world. He himself survived. He has a war-time diary (in Yiddish) that should be translated one day. My mother -- gentle, soft-spoken and kind -- was also a survivor. Her two daughters, my sisters, were machine-gunned in the village square of Rovno along with one hundred other relatives and friends.

My father has always been a model to me. Like him, I am a good raconteur, charming at times, withdrawn at others, but generally buoyant and optimistic. Like my mother, I am sensitive and gentle. Like my father, I am bold, outspoken and blunt. Like my mother, I too often have kept still. No longer. I must record who I am.

In my talks with Elie Wiesel, in his speeches and books, I have learned to become a witness. To understand myself is to understand my past. To remember the past is the path to self-realization. Remember the past -- not in order to suffer, but in order to liberate yourself and others -- toward a joyful exhilaration and exaltation of life. The Jew, as fighter and writer, must remember and record.

Norman Mailer has described the anger and alienation of modern men and women -- an anger that tears at the guts and destroys. For some this leads to psycho-somatic pathologies -- ulcers, indigestion, high blood pressure, an uneasy ennui; but for others, there is a need to channel that anger, like one sublimates sex or love or intimacy into sports, brutal play, drinking, dance, work, art, teaching or writing.

Writing, for me, was a controlled anger, a siphoning off of the sludge-fund of rage, a source of creative tension, into the conduits of authenticity. Now I am less angry but still searching. But writing is not enough for today's writer. You have to be an actor, a participant amidst the swirls of madness. You have to be on the Pentagon steps, at the Conspiracy trials, in Vietnam, Jerusalem, Harlem, in on the action, shaping political events as well as writing about them. You have to be a clown, a showman, a storyteller, an organizer, and all that to be a writer. If you're not a good showman, you have to at least be there on the spot, taking it all down. No more armchair historians, novelists and poets. You have to act, then record. You have to be your own witness and your own psychoanalyst.

Americans don't like to be told this, but you also have to be a competitive cutthroat, yet you can't tell the world you are. Norman Podhoretz, in his auto-biography Making It (Random House), perfectly describes this ambivalence.

One has to be cool. You have to be humble as you claw your way up towards success. A writer who lacks the proper humility is an open target. Mohammed Ali and Norman Mailer are two good examples. Everyone is eager to see their heads on the block. As Mailer says: "I'm the greatest; try to knock me off."

It's not "nice" to say that one writes to become well-known; to say that one loves to see his or her name in print; to say that one wants to be remembered, but that's at the core of most writers and intellec-tuals. Words are their only weapons. The worst punishment for a writer is to be ignored. Criticism? Fine. Controversy? Excellent. But to be ignored is a special hell reserved for the man and woman of letters.

Even radicals have the bourgeois goal of "making it." Only this time, it means "making it" against the establishment, rather than through it. Jerry Rubin, at the Conspiracy Trial, constantly scored his friend, Lee Weiner, the more academic rebel. "Lee, we're making history while all you're doing is writing your sociolo-gical thesis on revolution."

The radical also wants to be remembered. To ignore a radical, to ignore a writer, to ignore an intellectual is a terrible punishment.

In stating that I, too, hope to be remembered, even by a weak-eyed scholar in some dusty library a century from now, is to acknowledge that I have a spark of immortality in me. This may explain all the feverish writing that goes on today. There hangs over all of us the possibility of the Holocaust of Holocausts -- utter nuclear destruction. So the rule is live now, write now, love now, for tomorrow we all "die." The search for new ideas, new experiences, new thrills, new ecstasies, with no fullfillment, no security, no finality. Just a constant stream, barrage, of words and deeds, polluting the atmosphere, with no place to go, no home, no rest. All of it con-ditioned on the premise that we die like dogs, forgot-ten and ill-used.

The question then is: why be successful, ambitious, why be remembered, why go on with our jobs, our marriages, our loves, hates, pettinesses and dreams if it all blows up in the end anyway? I do not know. Maybe, because we feel that we alone will survive, that we alone will be one of the blessed; that someday they, whoever "they" are, will acknowledge "us," whoever "we" are.

We do what we do because we don't know what else to do. In any case, it takes up time. It keeps us going till we die. We don't think we have any other alternatives. To love and to work, Freud said, is really all we can do. We'll snatch a little happiness here, a little pain there, a bit of love, a smidgen of hate -- where we find it -- anywhere. Find someone. Find a guru, a teacher who knows something, anything, and follow him/her for a while till the novelty wears off, till something else comes along.

What we really lack is humility before God, before nature, and before the supernatural. We are too arrogant to admit that we are mere mortals, so we scream and rave and record our souls. We all wish to be witnesses...and survivors of the Holocaust of Holocausts.

We grow old too fast. We grow callous and sophisticated too soon. I should be saying what I'm saying now after I've lived a long life -- like at 80. I should be cynical like Freud at 80. But I know I won't change the world; I know I can change only one person -- me -- and maybe a few others. So I don't write to change the world but I write so as to understand myself.

There is a story in the Talmud about Lot and the people of Sodom and Gomorrah that tells the story. Lot wearily went about the streets preaching the end of the world to the sinners and the evil-doers, but no one listened. One man went up to Lot and asked: "Lot, why do you go around preaching to people to do good? They're not listening to you. They mock you. Why do you persist in your fruitless task?" And Lot wearily raised his head and said: "I preach not to change others, but rather that I will never become like them."

And that is the role of the writer today. Not only to make people feel again and experience again and remember again, but to feel, experience and remember

personally. Live your life, but don't become what you
mock.

---

*This book was never completed nor published. What did
appear was my collection of essays, which included
chapters on Jewish radicals like Marx and Marcuse, and
called <u>The Jew As Outsider</u>, University Press of
America, Lanham, Maryland, 1981.

1974

ISRAEL NEEDS A SOCIAL, POLITICAL,
AND PEACEFUL REVOLUTION

On the seventh day following the short but bloody Israel-Arab Six-Day War, there was no rest, no Shabbat (Sabbath). The cold-war thaw of the past half-decade has brought to the surface numerous social problems that were long waiting off-stage. A few sensitive Israelis had predicted that when peace "breaks out", there will be tzores (troubles). They are correct, but trouble has already begun -- even before an official peace has been declared.

Israel has a woman's movement; Israel has a consumer movement; Israel has a student protest movement; Israel has an anti-poverty movement; Israel has a civil and religious rights movement; and Israel has an ecology movement. Though they are tiny groups in most cases, they are, nevertheless, the vanguard of radical change, and these changes are long overdue.

Who could have predicated that Israel would ever have conscientious objectors to war? A Black Panther party? A Jewish Defense League? An Israeli New Left? A feminist movement? Israeli Jews engaging in espionage alongside Arabs? And these scandals and movements and forces for change will continue.

Recently, one of the leaders of the women's and consumer rights movement in Israel, Shulamit Aloni, a fifth-generation sabra, a lawyer, writer, and ex-Knesset member, visited the United States under the auspices of the Foreign Ministry. In one of her speeches, she said:

"I understand our leaders (in Israel). After all, how many battles can they be asked to fight in a lifetime? They fought before they came and again after they came. They're old and tired. They deserve to have peace within our borders, but that is impossible. Change is imperative."

I agree 1000 percent (forgive me, Senator Eagleton). The present Israeli leadership is old -- Golda Meir is 75; Zalman Shazar and David Ben-Gurion are over 80; Pinchas Sapir and other Cabinet members are long past retirement age. But age is not the issue because there are clear-eyed and far-sighted visionaries among the "old-guard". The real need is for progressive and provident leadership. The crucial problem in Israel is how to get beyond the "garrison state" mentality that permeates the state.

Before there can be any meaningful radical change internally, there must be peace with the Arab state externally. This is not the place for a far-ranging analysis of this emotional and controversial topic, but I must say that one step toward that goal of peace is the recognition of the Palestinian people's aspiration for a homeland. My position is that a bi-national state (really a tri- or quatro-national state, because too often, Christians, both Arab and non-Arab, and Druzes, are forgotten) is a futile and naive dream. No, a bi-national "workers" state will not work. The only real alternative is a Palestinian state in what is now Jordan.

If you ask me what I really believe, I will say that I am extremely pessimistic; this hot and cold war that now exists will continue for my lifetime; I anxiously await any change in the status-quo, no matter how insignificant, but overall I am not very hopeful about peace. The entire stalemate depresses me terribly, but I wait.... As for now, I am concerned about Israeli society.

As I've emphasized, Israel needs new progressive leadership; the Knesset needs more women, more young people, more Arabs, more Sephardim, more Westerners (especially more Americans with an innovative spirit), but especially it needs far-sighted progressive leadership!

The Israeli government, though it has undertaken miracles in absorption, land and water development, and education, is insensitively over-bureaucratized, as any Ephraim Kishon story portrays. The Israeli leadership, a product of intensive change, is now threatened by change, and its reactions on some issues have shown, not only the cracks and fissures within the social fabric of Israel, but also the government's myopic, and at times, repressive policies. For example:

a) Golda Meir once called the Israeli Black Panther Party, "a bunch of delinquents." Compare this with what another leader, Elie Eliacher, said in January 1972 at an assembly of Sephardic delegates to the 28th Zionist Congress, attended by many top officials and religious leaders:

"Two Israels cannot survive. Our history has proved it. We cannot afford to have one happy, prosperous Israel reaping all the advantages of our eventful period while another Israel lacks the most elementary conditions of life, living in slums, underfed, underclothed, struggling on an income close to the dole, unrepresented in our national forums.... The Black Panther movement is only a symptom of things to come which can and must at all costs be prevented."

b) The high-handed blockage of the long-sympathetic Arabs of Baram and Ikrit to return to their fields and homes.

c) Amos Kenan, controversial Israeli journalist, has had his play censored because the government is offended.

d) Lillith, a critical English-language journal edited by (mostly American) students living in Jerusalem, is censured because a comic strip by David Geva -- called "Super Golda", with Premier Meir caricatured as a tough "super-man" -- incurred the wrath of an Israeli bureaucrat.

These and other examples should point out to the reader that much more attention must be paid to internal social problems and to internal civil liberties, despite the concerns of aliya (immigration), klita (absorption of immigrants), bitachon (security), and development.

Change is possible in Israel. It has a democratic socialist tradition. It has (I strongly hope) the flexibility and apparatus for social change. It has a tradition of civil rights for minorities. It has a Halacha that must be flexible enough to adjust and adapt to a new world, a world of rapid and dizzying change, a world entering "future shock".

Like all modernizing nations, Israel is following, in many ways, the American pattern of development: consumerism, a higher standard of living, plus all the problems that highly technological societies face -- pollution, urban decay, increased population, inadequate housing and transportation, a widening gap between the rich and the poor, alienation and post-affluence social movements -- drugs, juvenile delinquency, counter-culture sects, anxious minority groups who want to enter the "good life" or a productive life beyond mere material goods.

-14-

I see Israel where America was in the early 60's. Nevertheless it is in much better shape than America to solve its problems and to integrate its dissident minority movements. But will it? Or will it react in a crass and unyielding manner? When Golda Meir called the Black Panther Party in Israel a "bunch of delinquents," I knew then that Israel was in trouble and my estimation of Ms. Meir's political acumen plummeted.

Israel needs new leadership. It needs new ways to protect human rights; it needs to allow peaceful dissent and even a bit of disruption; it needs to listen well to the voices of protest; it needs to adopt a constitution and a bill of rights (it has neither) granting civil liberties; it needs to change the legal structure of marriage and divorce to adapt to a new life-style; it needs to increase and enforce human rights, especially for women and especially in the area of jobs, marriage, and divorce.

Israel must undertake the excruciating task of deciding what kind of state it wants to be -- a secular Jewish state, an orthodox theocracy, or some viable compromise?

Many Jews, both in the diaspora and in Israel, will oppose the tide of social change. Some have said --"What's so pressing about women's rights or consumerism? There are more important issues. We need to collect money for national security." This sentiment is expressed by many American Jewish leaders. Though money is extremely important, it is not the solution to every problem.

I am reminded of the words of the late great Martin Luther King, Jr.: "Philanthropy is commendable, but it must not cause the philanthropist to overlook the circumstances of economic injustice which makes philanthropy necessary."

These words are too often forgotten by men of wealth. These Jewish leaders (and their wives) do not even recognize their own male chauvinism and anti-feminist emotions. (In Israel, they would be called, "basar lavan", Hebrew for "white meat," because chauvinist pig is not kosher.)

These movements, especially those dealing with women's rights (divorce, marriage, etc.) will be staunchly opposed by religious traditionalists, who feel that separation of synagogue and state would be disastrous and would undermine and completely "eliminate" religion. Civil divorce and marriage plus equal rights for women would only reflect the reality of the state -- a state in which over 50 percent of the citizens (the majority) are <u>not</u> Orthodox, yet are coerced to abide present rulings. There should be civil as well as religious marriages and divorces. The choice should be left up to the individual, not the state.

It is said that since the destruction of the Temple, only fools make predictions. Still, I would predict that the majority of citizens would still have Orthodox religious marriage rites. Only a few would opt for civil marriages, but it would be the individual's choice, not the state's.

The major reason why religious traditionalists will oppose the civil and women's rights movements is because <u>religion and politics are intertwined in Israel</u>.

The religious parties will oppose these movements not simply on grounds of <u>Halacha</u>, but for reasons of <u>realpolitik</u>. They stand to lose enormous political and economic power if civil liberties are extended to everyone, regardless of race, sex, religion, or national origin. Therefore, I can well understand their opposition -- it is the <u>sine qua non</u> of power. They might lose control of the enormous religious apparatus that has developed -- the rabbinical courts, the slaughterhouses, the <u>mohelim</u> (ritual circumcizers), the religious schools, and yeshivot.

In short, what makes the conflict so difficult and so deserving of the wisdom of a Solomon, is simply because of this double-barreled problem of loss of political power <u>and</u> infringement of <u>Halacha</u>.

I call for a radical transformation within Israeli society. I am not a political organizer, and I am not an Israeli citizen. This internal revolution can only be undertaken by Jewish, Arab, Christian, and Druze citizens within the Israeli state. I am simply an intellectual and an outside social critic, writing from afar. This article is <u>not</u> a detailed political program; it is <u>not</u> a precise manual for strategic intervention; it is simply a "call to arms", a declaration for action, action that I believe is long overdue.

I do, however, have a few "guidelines". The term, revolution, is used in a variety of ways. Some equate it with any profound social and political change. Some with a "storming of the palace" form of coup d'etat. Others in a more restrictive sense use the term to mean an attack on the moral-political order and the traditional hierarchy of class statuses which commences when existing institutions lose their legitimacy and can no longer function without widescale repression.

The concept of revolution is very broad and this short discussion will not do it justice. But in short, what is necessary is a long-term, concerted, political and economic action combined with innovative cultural change -- revolutionizing the way people live in their daily lives and the way they relate intimately with each other. This is not revolution in the historic meaning of the term, but a slow drive for radical change using both traditional and novel means. Or as radical theoretician Richard Flacks has described it:

> The revolution in advanced society is not a single insurrection. It is not a civil war of pitched battles fought by opposing armies. It is a long, continuous struggle -- with political, social, and cultural aspects inextricably interwined.... It is not simply a socialist revolution, if by that one means the establishment of a new form of state power...It is more than that. For it must be a revolution of those whose lives are determined by those decisions. It is, in short, not a revolution aimed at seizing power but a revolution aimed at its dispersal.

One last point: Many Jews wish to muzzle criticism of Israel or feel that any deep critique of Israel plays into the hands of its enemies. To these Jews, I ask them to listen intently to the words of Noam Chomsky, who, in a recent Ramparts (January, 1973) article, wrote the following:

> Surely it is obvious that a critical analysis of Israeli institutions and practices does not simply imply antagonism to the people of Israel, denial of the national rights of the Jews in Israel, or lack of concern for their just aspirations and needs. The demand for equal rights for Palestinians (as well as women, Sephardim, etc.) does not imply a

-17-

demand for Arab dominance...or a denial of Jewish rights. The same is true of critical analysis that questions the existence of the state institutions in their present form.

* * * *

I call for a social, political, and non-violent revolution in Israel, a kind of (Charles) Reichian "greening" of Israel. To some this demand seems incredible; to others, it smacks of treason. Yet, I make this demand because I _love_ Israel, and I criticize Israel because I _love_ it. To silence criticism is to silence freedom. This is _my_ message to Israel on its 25th Anniversary.

1973

Milwaukee, the middle of Middle America. A quiet and strange city in a strange state. A state with a tradition of progressive political ideals going back to "Fighting Bob" Lafollette, going back to socialist mayors like Frank Ziedler and the panjandrum of Wisconsin socialism, Victor Berger. But it's also a state that has produced Senator Joseph McCarthy and gave George Wallace a lot of votes. Figure that out. The contradictions of America are reflected in Wisconsin.

Milwaukee. The city of beer, bratwurst, and the Braves. The Braves moved to Atlanta; the bratwurst to Sheboygan, and the beer moved out to St. Louis via Budweiser. But, don't get me wrong, Milwaukee still has beer (and brats). The descendents of the old families -- Pabst, Schlitz, Miller -- still run the town, but Milwaukee lost the beer-drinking award to Cleveland a while back.

Milwaukee. A beautiful and clean city. Milwaukee. The biggest little village in the world. It's so small that whenever I go downtown, I never fail to meet at least one friend. Try that in New York, Chicago or L.A. Yet it's got nearly a million people. A metropolis with big-city problems and small-town gemutleich-keit.

Like Chicago or Cleveland, Milwaukee is still a city composed of "little villages" -- neighborhoods that retain their ethnic/racial distinction. Irish, Italians, Germans, Poles, Russians, Slovaks, Greeks, Swedes, Slovenes, Lithuanians, Jews, Puerto Ricans, Chinese, Japanese, Mexicans, Cubans, and Afro-Americans. During the two decades directly before and directly after the turn of the century, the country filled up with Europeans from the East; Japanese and Chinese from the West; and Blacks (Negroes then) from the South. They came to do the dirty work in the tanneries, meat packing plants, foundries, steel mills, and shoe factories.

There's a railroad line that runs like a thin curved ribbon from Ellis Island in New York north up to Albany, Schnectady, and Syracuse (another ribbon cuts across Pennsylvania) and onto Rochester, Buffalo, Cleveland, Toledo, Detroit, Gary, Hammond, Chicago and on up to Milwaukee. The white ethnics dropped off along the line to find their brothers and sisters and stayed to set up their ethnic villages.

Milwaukee is like Chicago _fin de siecle_. In fact, when Hollywood director Norman Jewison looked for locations of Chicago in 1900 for his film _Gaily, Gaily_, he went to Milwaukee -- to "east town", near the river. It's still got an old world feel to it.

Milwaukee. People keep busy in the summer with Fourth of July Circus Parades, Summerfest, the State Fair. An old-fashioned town. A good town to grow up in. I should know. I spent a very happy childhood there, doctor, and a miserable adolescence.

This is the tale of my coming back to Milwaukee, the return of the native, back to my junior and senior high school, and culminating in my high school's tenth year anniversary reunion. It's quite a trip: 1962-1972. Quite a decade. Rivals 1929-1939 for top honors in cataclysmic events. I think it beats the thirties, but I don't know. I wasn't there. To paraphrase Will Rogers, I only now what I see on T.V., and I saw about 2,000 hours of reality on the "boob tube" during that decade. And as we used to say in the fifties, I saw some pretty neat things.

* * * *

One night in 1964, Earl L. B. Clark, the principal of Steuben Junior High School on Milwaukee's northwest side, locked his garage doors, got into a car, turned on the motor and killed himself.

The natural question we all asked ourselves was ... why?

It was like out of Edwin Arlington Robinson's "Richard Corey." Why would this tall, impeccably dressed, self-composed man want to kill himself? I had to find out, and the answer that emerged was a profound statement on the nature of America's educational system.

In a sense, Earl L. B. Clark was as much a victim of the swirl and madness of social movements in the sixties as were King, Kennedy, and the Kent State Four.

I graduated from Steuben in 1959. Looking back, the fifties seemed like a dream world. Elvis Presley.

Dion and the Belmonts. Dick Clark. The Platters.
Fabian. Annette Funichello. Buddy Holly. Davy
Crockett. Hulahoops. Sputnik. Payola. The $64,000
Questions. Scandola. Sunday afternoon movies with ten
cartoons, two westerns, the Three Stooges, and a
Captain Midnight Serial. Bosco. Howdy Doody, Buffalo
Bob, and the Show of Shows.

At "sock hops" and chaperoned proms, we danced the
jitterbug and the stroll. At parties we drank coke,
ate potato chips, and played spin-the-bottle and post-
office. At the playground, we shot ringers, played
kickball and "strike-out," and hoped to win the city
softball championship. (We lost.)

A lot of fond memories. The 50's were great for a
thirteen year old kid. Too young for politics. I
didn't even know who Adlai Stevenson was until my folks
said they'd vote for him because he was a nice guy.
Lost twice, I heard.

But school was the focal point. We played hard
and we studied even harder. In junior high school, the
school was split between the "greasers" and the
"collegiates." The latter were getting primed for
college; the former were primed for the technical
schools. Maybe there was no formal tracking in the
schools, but in the end, the results were the same.

The "collegiates" studied their asses off, joined
what seemed like an interminable number of after-school
clubs, and stood in nice straight lines with polite
smiles on their faces. The "greasers" goofed off, got
into fights, took most of the mechanical arts classes,
and were sent down to the principal's (really the
vice-principal's) office with regularity.

Steuben was one of the many feeder schools that
supplied Washington High School with students. Just as
you can judge a college by the quality of its high
schools; so too can you judge a high school by the
quality of its junior high schools ... and Steuben had
good quality students.

The "greasers" were a small but exotic group; the
majority of students, the "collegiates" came from
solidly middle-class Jewish or German families and
were, in educational jargon, highly motivated. Or
better, they were overly-motivated. Both our parents'
desires and the post-Sputnik race to outdistance the

-21-

Russians propelled many, if not all of us, to "make it."

Between 1950 and early 1960, Washington High School was considered one of the finest high schools in the city. After graduating from Steuben, I entered into those final glory years. When I graduated from Washington in 1962, I didn't know it then but we were to be considered one of the last of the "great' classes. From 1962 on, Washington and, of course, Steuben began to go downhill ... or so the teachers and administrators told us.

My years at Washington from 1959 to 1962 were more of the same: sports, dating, school clubs, and hitting the books. We all scrambled for the top grades, the top honors (National Honor Society), and the top elected offices whether in Boys' Club, Tonia Toppers, or the Lincoln Debating Society.

The big men in school were of course the "lettermen," with their white sweaters festooned with red W's, gold and silver medals, and other paraphernalia. Next in status seemed to be the cheerleaders. Down the list came the "scholars", the grinds who won top honor awards or got straight A's, and further down were the rest of the students. Holding down the bottom but still well-respected were the "greasers" -- the sharp, slick, tough (to us) chicks and guys who were in their own way, the first rebels, the first hippies.

Nearly all the collegiates went on to college, some even to Harvard or Oberlin. Many went to Madison and another large portion went on the UWM. The girls were going on to college to find husbands; some went to work; some were getting married; some (the scandal of it) were secretly married and pregnant. The star basketball player (later to become a Milwaukee cop) was to marry the star cheerleader, have a kid a few months after the ceremony, and supposedly live happily ever after. (They didn't.)

As for the "greasers", some were to go into the army (this was before Vietnam and the draft); or into construction jobs; or get an apprenticeship for a trade, or do other things that "greasers" do. A few, rumor had it, had been in jail; and one or two were being groomed to take over some Mafia position.

Of politics we knew or cared little. The only event even smacking of politics was the time that a few of us protested to the principal that somebody was passing out John Birch Society literature in the halls, and we felt that an editorial should be written about it in the school paper.

We meekly walked into the principal's office and began to debate the issue. At first the principal agreed to the editorial and then reneged. As we started to methodically point out the inconsistencies in his argument, he got angry and threw us out of his office! At that time, students, like Blacks, had to know their place. One didn't argue with a teacher or principal; one just accepted their final decrees like acts of God.

I graduated from Washington in 1962, traveled through Europe and Israel for a year, and in 1963 entered the University of Wisconsin-Milwaukee (UW-M) just as Camelot was about to fall. The Cuban missile crisis set the stage of paranoia; Kennedy was assassinated; the Civil Rights movement was in full swing; Vietnam became more than just a strange name to stamp collectors; the revolt was on.

While I was at UW-M, I heard about Clark's suicide. It bothered me; I had liked the man. But there were too many other distractions; Watts, Newark, Detroit, the War, Women, and, of course, school.

I graduated from the University of Wisconsin in June 1967, a day before the Israeli-Arab Six-Day War, and two weeks before my first (and last) acid trip. Graduate school at Northwestern in sociology began and continued on into the 70's. I had flunked my physical at the army induction center so I just stayed in school. The tumult of the last decade carried on but as the movement quieted down, I had some time to reflect on the past decade and was drawn back to my old schools to see the changes that had gone down ... the suicide of Earl L. B. Clarke being the touchstone.

I returned to Washington and Steuben during the past year to do some investigating. Things had changed; there were no dress codes; there were many Blacks and Chicanos (there was only one lonely black "dude" when I graduated); there was smoke in the johns; and a general aura of paranoia.

In fact, on my first trip back, I had trouble even getting into the school -- all visitor's passes were

revoked. I saw my old gym teacher and he let me in,
but told me I couldn't take any pictures.

I didn't stay long, but from the short time I was
there, I noticed the tension and subdued anger on the
faces of the teachers. I started rapping with the gym
teacher, now an assistant principal.

"You see those kids (pointing to a few Blacks out
on the sidewalk), they should be in class. Damn it,
things were different ten years ago. The colored come
in now and all the rules have to change just to please
them."

I felt sorry for him and a bit angry. In a way,
he seemed like Archie Bunker, someone who could have
easily become a cop if he hadn't gone into teaching.
Ten years ago, he was just a gym teacher; now he looked
like a brave warrier holding down the line for law and
order. It seemed as if he had learned nothing from the
rebellion of the last decade; he understood nothing.
It seemed that the students had changed, the times had
changed, but the teachers had not, even the school with
its rows of lockers and wooden desks, had been kept
intact, like a museum piece.

He told me of the fires at the school, the false
alarms, the drugs, the flexing of student power, the
questioning of authority, the breakdown of rules. His
world was crumbling around him, and he didn't know how
or why it was happening.

I walked into the vice-principal's office. To my
surprise, he immediately recognized me. After some
perfunctory cordiality, he said:

"Your class was one of the last of the good ones;
now, there's just trouble."

More sadness, more tales of gloom. I was an outsider now. With me he talked of the old days, the
really quiet good old days. But the tension was there
in the creases of his face. A month later, I read in
the paper, he died of a heart attack. Another
casualty.

Not long after my visit to Washington, I went back
to Steuben. The Clark suicide was still on my mind.

Steuben was an all-white school a decade or less
ago; today there were Blacks, Chicanos, Puerto Ricans,

and Indians, but still it was predominately white, maybe 70 percent.

Suddenly, the bell rang and teachers with their students were rushing outside. I thought it was the bell between classes; it was a false alarm. I ducked into the principal's offie and looked around. A secretary came up to me and asked if I wanted to see the principal.

I said I'd like to talk to someone and that I had been a Steuben graduate and all. Well, the principal was out (that seemed to be true ten years ago too --the principal was always out -- where, no one knew or wanted to tell.)

The secretary asked if I would like to see the vice-principal. I said sure, I knew him back when he was just a music teacher. He had moved up in the world. I walked into his office.

A replay of Washington. More gloom, more crises, more tension.

"I feel like a cop," he said as he twirled in his seat to answer to phone for the third time in about ten minutes. "No time to teach, just discipline."

"You've heard about the problems at Washington?" I nodded.

"Here it's not that bad, but it's bad enough. We had some disturbances a while back. A lot of broken windows."

He went on to explain that the students didn't like the rules concerning the closed lunch sessions. They couldn't eat their lunch on the playground or go off into the streets and businesses surrounding the playground to eat or just rap so they broke 200 windows.

"I may be old-fashioned, but I feel a rule is a rule and rules should be obeyed."

"I put the blame on the parents, the stability of the home. When you were here, the parents complained that we didn't give enough homework. Today everyone complains we give too much."

"We had solid middle-class families here a while back, now there's no stability. I've got a report that shows that 55 percent of the families that send their kids here have only one parent at home."

The alcove outside his office was filling up with kids -- nice looking kids who were going to get "disciplined." And I thought, where were the "greasers?" Now, even "nice kids" were rebelling.

"There's been more vandalism in the past six months than in the past ten years combined and I blame the parents. We shouldn't be doing their job."

More calls. More trouble. I brought up the question of Clarke's suicide. With an unexpected bluntness, he told me.

"Clark was a good man, but he just couldn't adjust. He couldn't roll with the punches."

The contagion had spread, from the colleges down to the high schools and now the junior highs. The rebellion was against the sense of powerlessness, against the "bullshit" taught in the schools, against the formidable rules. There were new alternatives, alternatives unavailable to us ten years ago. And you had to move with times or go under the wheel.

I concluded the rap, told him I'd try to come back. It was 10:30. Another false alarm went off, the second of the morning. I followed the merry horde and their nervous teachers out the door and into the street.

I probably won't come back.

* * * *

Betty Maris was worried. She had put a lot of work into this reunion -- Washington High Schools' 10th Year Anniversary Reunion -- June 1962 to June 1972. A lot happened during those ten years to me, to this country, and to Betty.

Betty, a pretty Greek girl, once a star cheerleader now a school teacher, was disappointed with the group that crowded into a dining room of the spanking new Performing Arts Center. I didn't think it was a disappointing crowd, (maybe because I was too "stoned"), but later I was told that only 26 percent of the class had showed up, 138 out of 545 alumni.

Some didn't have the money, (cost: $20 a couple, plus parking, baby-sitter, etc.) or didn't want to spend it. Some lived too far away. Some probably wanted to come, but maybe a spouse objected. One woman, another popular cheerleader, didn't show up because she was too ashamed to admit that she was still <u>unmarried</u>. Some were dead. Some were in Vietnam or overseas. Some were taking law boards or final exams. Most, however, might have thought that it would have been a neat nostalgic "trip," but their lives had changed to the point where they had little in common with their former classmates.

While the band played, I sauntered over to the bar and looked around. Our "class" looked good -- healthy and well-groomed. Not too many had gone to "pot." For some, this was the biggest event of the year, maybe of

the past ten. Some had little else but fine memories of carefree high school days. Frustrations, dead-end jobs, rotten luck, all would be forogtten for a few golden hours.

The class president, as jovial as a Junior Chamber of Commerce officer, had shed over 100 pounds. I hardly recognized the guy. Another ex-cheerleader, Bonnie Braun, was the envy of all the women with her sleek figure. She was now a world-hopping airline stewardess and had married well, a wealthy California man ten years her senior.

I began rapping with another ex-cheerleader (I knew them all). Gail, after three children, looked great and was as sexy as ever. Her husband, a former basketball star, was now a crew-cut, tight-lipped, overweight cop. He glared down at me all the while I drank with his wife, jealous that this "pointy-headed intellectual writer" could entertain <u>his</u> wife. The more others ogled; the more her husband scowled; the more Gail loved it.

The class had produced about ten marriages and they were all intact. Two women still had a "flame" going with guys they had met during high school days and ten years later they were still waiting and hoping to get married to them. They're still waiting.

Dinner was served. I sat at a table with the relatively successful -- lawyers, doctors, junior executives. We even had a "guest appearance" of a fellow who composed musical scores for T.V. and Broadway -- Dennis Hanley (nee Hirshbein). A celebrity!

As a writer and political activist, I regaled my attentive audience with tales of publishers, literary agents, and the New York "scene." Mostly, they listened as I described the March on Washington, the "armies of the night," the Chicago "conspiracy" trial, the 1968 Democratic convention, and all the other rocking shocking events of the 60's.

I feared a blacklash, but these were the sons and daughters of a "middle America' that had seen it and lived it vicariously with Walter Cronkite and now with me. They added their tales to the memories I spun for them, and we all relished them together.

The entertainment began. The president of the class welcomed us and talked on in cliches - "we were a class devoted to service; we must continue to serve our community." Middle America wasn't listening. The T.V. composer was asked to sing and sing he did in a beautiful, trained voice. The remnants of the football team at the back table weren't listening. Too drunk. An ex-Vietnam veteran now turned "hippy-freak-radical," dressed incongruously in black and green jungle camouflage suit, sang "Oh, Shenandoah". At this point, even I wasn't listening.

The crowd didn't want entertainment; they wanted booze ... T.V. they could watch at home. Now, they wanted talk and gusty tales of the Green Bay Packers and their rival gridiron teams.

There were a few prizes. For the most children (six in ten years). The winner waddled up. For the longest hair. The Vietnam vet and I both lost to a "dark horse" candidate. We didn't even recognize the dude. He could have walked in off the street. For the farthest distance traveled. (Nam and Guam and Laos didn't count.) One guy, a doctor jumped up and shouted "Israel." A girl meekly intoned "Alaska". Alaska sounded more plausible, but "Israel" demanded an open hearing at this United-Nations-of-Middle-America. This dude wanted the award so badly -- just like he was sucking for national honors society or student government. He got it -- a booby prize - a three-foot high styrofoam replica of the Liberty Bell.

After thanking the reunion committee, and after exchanging addresses with people we knew we'd never call again, we all stood up to sing the school anthem -- with all the de riguer foot-stomping and giggling that goes along with anachronistic cultural play-backs.

It was time to leave. The bar had run out of booze.

* * * *

A few months after the reunion, I went up to talk to Ron Franzmeier, the ex-class prez, now assistant to the president of Manpower, Inc., in Milwaukee, its international center. Ron is really a nice guy, and service to the community is no cliche to him. He lives it.

"You know - reunions are dying out," he told me as he leaned back in his swivel chair. "The change is due to our temporary relationships between people," he added. (Alvin Toffler would call it "modular life styles.)

"Graduates in the 30's and 40's know where people live and how they are. They still socialize. When they travel, they stop for dinner, even from San Francisco or New York, but our class doesn't do this anymore. People just don't develop those lasting relationships anymore."

Sadly, he noted: "We live in a temporary society and I work for a company that epitomizes all this -- temporary work. Our president Elmer Winter (of Manpower, Inc.) says that very few people receive 25 year gold watches anymore. Young people today don't show many signs of making a career in one company. There's too much jumping around."

"High school played a more significant role in the 30's and 40's. In those days, the senior prom, the yearbook, the graduation ceremony were the highlights of their young lives. Today, with more kids going to college, high school is just a steppingstone rather than a finale, so it's not that important anymore. Subsequently, reunions aren't so important or success-ful anymore, either."

It goes even deeper. In a McLuhanesque world, there is a greater variety of stimuli outside the school. As Ron Franzmeier puts it:

"How can a school play or a debating team compete with a war in your own living room? Today, there's no debate on capital punishment, you just go out and picket!"

Ron Franzmeier is now the Director of the Washington High School Scholarship Foundation, which was founded in 1961, and in which he was one of the first winners when we graduated back in 1962. He noted that the "troubles" at Washington made it much more difficult to collect funds, but things have improved.

"The older alumni now understand the school and understand the changes a lot better. They feel relieved that the school is changing in a positive way and not being destroyed. We now give out eight $500 scholarships a year. They've toured the school, talked to students, white and black, and while still unhappy with some changes, still, the crisis has rallied them to continue to support us. Their own kids go here too."

* * * *

What exactly happened to Washington High School? The scenario is a familiar one. In 1962, there were one or two black students. Then, bussing started. Integration was the watchword in the years 1963-1964. In short, the 25 percent middle-class Jewish minority was replaced by a 20 percent Black minority. It was an old story in the 1960's. A clash of life styles, of racial strife, and of student power. It's a national phenomenon.

One feeder school, Steuben Junior High, was predominantly white working class. Another feeder school, Peckham, was mostly Black working class. When they converged on Washington, trouble began.

But as a Washington-watcher for all these years, I'm happy to report that the worst is over ... I hope. In fact, wherever I went and to whomever I talked, everyone told me to write positively of the changes that have occurred.

This past year I've seen how one school coped with change. There's hope. There's a new and younger prin-

-30-

cipal at Washington; there are new and "hipper" teachers; there is stronger community, alumni, and student participation.

Two voluntary associations that have helped are the Parent-Teacher-Student Association (replacing the old PTA) and a local neighborhood group, the Sherman Park Community Association.

The SPCA's concern goes beyond just school strife, but into action over expressway construction, housing patterns, attempted block-busting, and other issues. It even promotes block parties and youth outings. It is one of many such associations springing up across the country. Its major goal: to create a sense of community and neighborhood involvement in order to slow down the rampage of the "temporary, modular society."

Washington has now become more of a vocationally-oriented school than in the years I went. It still meets the needs of the college-bound, but, in addition, offers exposure to the trades (electrician, welder, plumber).

One exciting example: a nearby service station owned by the school gives students credit in auto mechanics and business managing. Ex-welders and ex-electricians now teach the kids. Students work on an entire corner of a house in the schools' workshops.

All reports show that vocational-technical training is increasing; while college attendance has dipped slightly. A college graduate is no longer assured a job. There are hundreds unemployed, including many Ph.D's. A voc-tech graduate has a better chance for a job today than his college peer.

The strain has been great on teachers. Many have left to teach elsewhere, seeking the white middle-class students they know and loved in the past. Those that remain and who have adapted to the "culture shock" are now working harder than ever to keep old standards alive, but the interest just isn't there.

Teachers had to be re-educated to cope with Black culture, to cope with the youth culture. Some, like Earl L. B. Clark, couldn't do it. Others try and muddle through. Still others are bitter, very bitter.

As one teacher put it: "I've become radicalized. I don't believe in integration anymore. Teachers should teach their own kind. If Blacks want Black teachers, Black curriculum, Black administrators, Black anything -- I say give it to them. Let them run their own schools in their own way. I've had it up to here. I'd rather teach white kids. In fact, I'd rather teach Jewish kids; Black should teach Blacks; Catholics should teach Catholics; and Jews should teach Jews!" (The teacher was Jewish, by the way.)

Through all the bitterness and chaotic change of the past decade, there is hope. As one teacher put it: "If we don't make it at Washington, I don't know where we will."

Washington in a small way has "made it." The rioting has ceased; the halls are fairly quiet; there are fewer cigarettes snuffed out in the carpet; there is more student power. This could all be reversed tomorrow but today, it's quiet.

Ron Franzmeier says "Students may have less res- pect and less sentimental attachment to a school but they now have a place that serves their needs."

The long hard march through the institutions of this society is still far from over, but amidst the cynicism, there's always faith. We've been left with little else.

Amidst My Lai, the Pentagon Papers, the Watergate Scandal, and all the rest, Washington High School (and I) survived the 60's. We've made it through, and if we've made it, then there's still some hope for the rest of the nation.

1973

THE MAKING OF A SOCIOLOGIST

Introduction

This is an impressionistic memoir of my four years of graduate study at Northwestern University from 1967-1971, and deals with personal and professional conflicts in such matters as academic socialization, sex roles, political tensions, Black-white relations, psychological and sexual tensions, religious ambivalences, and life style conflicts. It concludes with a question that all people, not only sociologists, must answer: to whom do you owe your life? to your teachers? your parents? or ultimately to yourself? Hopefully, the essay will also serve two other functions: to formulate policy and encourage more humane means of socializing graduate students; and secondly, to encourage research in the areas raised in this article; in short, to convert these personal impressions into hard data. I certainly hope so because I believe the issues raised here have not disappeared.

Looking back at those years in Evanston, Illinois, they were not only four very turbulent years in American political history but four very special years in my social and intellectual growth. These memoirs are really vignettes of a time and place that will never be duplicated again. It has taken nearly a dozen years to cut the so-called "academic umbilical cord" and to gain needed perspective. Yet, when I look back, the memory, while filled with moments of pain, is also permeated with warmth and intellectural excitement. Such intense social, emotional, and intellectual excitement rarely comes again after graduate school. For me the sociology department emerges as a relatively humane place despite the personal turmoil, political tensions, and personality clashes. The university has traditionally been a place to shake-up preconceived attitudes, and the late 60's was quite a time for "shaking-up".

Northwestern University (herein to be called NU), the only private school of the Big-Ten Conference, was also a relatively small one compared to such academic "factories" as the University of Wisconsin, Illinois, Minnesota, or Michigan. This gave us a welcome intimacy. Furthermore, although we sometimes fell under the shadow of our illustrious neighbor down the lake, the University of Chicago (U. of C.), I remember several Chicago graduate students telling me how they envied the close-knit relationship between faculty, students, and staff at NU. This was missing to some degree at U. of C.

In terms of prestige, graduate students from both schools respected each other and sometimes dated each other.[1]

The Faculty and Its Impact

I was blessed with a fine, fairly young faculty at NU and they did much to turn us into good sociologists. While there were differences of opinion on this issue (as I will discuss later), several important contributions were made by students later. I'd like to briefly describe some of our teachers and their impact.

As in most departments, students gravitated to various sociological styles and methods. For example, if one wished to specialize in the sociology of deviance, occupations, and the "soft" methods of participant observation, one tried to have Howard S. Becker on one's dissertation committee. Becker, to me, was one of the most charismatic figures in the department. A student of Everett C. Hughes at U. of C., he had done work on musicians, teachers, and marijuana smokers that was considered quite radical at the time. If his labeling theory of deviance is now somewhat "old-hat", in the 1950's and 1960's it was innovative and exciting. I still marvel at his teaching abilities in methods class; no notes, cigarette dangling from his mouth, he could make the most insightful comments about the most mundane occupations. His work was theoretical but based firmly on much first-hand observation. He, and his celebrated colleague in labeling theory, John Kitsuse, influenced many of us. Two students in particular who have continued in this sociological tradition are Malcolm Spector of McGill University and Charles Suchar of De Paul University of Chicago.

Becker, a man constantly on the move intellectually, perhaps forsaw the decline of interest in labeling theory (or else he felt "talked-out" on the subject), and in my last year at NU began to move in a field that was beginning to attract attention -- the sociology of art, and he and his students (Barbara Rosenbloom of Stanford University and Chandra Hecht

Mukerji, now at the University of California - San Diego) made initial contributions to this area, especially in the sociology of photography and theatre. Becker had the gift of knowing when to move on to new and exciting vistas and to take a few students along with him.

Others: in the field of urban studies, one gravitated to Scott Greer, Arnold Feldman, and Janet Abu-Lughod; in the sociology of law, to Richard Schwartz, who later became the first sociologist to head a law school (at the State University of New York - Buffalo); in the sociology of the military and developing nations, to Charles (Charlie) Moskos and Arnold Feldman; in demography, to Allan Schnaiberg and Janet Abu-Lughod; in African social organization, education and the family, to Remi Clignet; in family studies, to the late Robert Winch; and for social stratification, education, and minority relations, to Raymond Mack.

Bernard Beck, a specialist in many areas (theory, religion, welfare) though not a prolific writer, was important to me and other students both for his formidable knowledge in the history of sociological thought and for his warm personal style which attracted many of us to his office for coffee and talk. The late Robert Winch, while older and more austere, taught me quantitative methods though his real interest lie in survey research on the family. Several of his students went on to make a name: Rae Lesser Blumberg and Louis Wolf Goodman. It was a terribly sad loss when this tall, stately, handsome man died of cancer a few years ago. Richard Berk and Carol Owens were also influential in small ways. They were junior faculty at the tail-end of my years at NU. I might add that the chairmen of the department during 1967-1971 were Ray Mack, Robert Winch, and Charles Moskos. Mack did not make too much of an impression on me since he moved into the administration of NU and was rarely around. Charlie Moskos became a good friend, and while some students disagreed with his views on Vietnam and the military, his courses on political sociology were memorable. In all, we had good young scholars and seasoned veterans and most were excellent teachers. I might add that NU had teachers in other departments that I took courses with: Donald Campbell and Jack Sawyer in psychology, Edward Hall in anthropology, and several in film and Africana studies.

Northwestern produced a number of fine scholars active in the field: Ron Edari (social change); Steve

Buff, Joyce Kozuch, Arthur Paris (Caribbean and Black Studies); Sam Mueller (sociology of religion); George Kourvetaris (military sociology); Joseph Blake (collective behavior); Margaret Gordon, Paul Lubeck, William Bridges (labor studies); and several others, including some active in foreign affairs: Bic Ijomah, Pasquale Payanza, Jose Gil, and Luis Salces.[2]

Without being overly modest, I too have made a contribution in the area of racial and ethnic minorities, the sociology of Jewry, Israeli politics, the sociology of genocide; Jewish radicalism, and conflict/ conflict resolution. A book based on my dissertation topic, Student Protest and the Technocratic Society: The Case of ROTC (1973), and an anthology that has become very influential in its field, Jewish Radicalism: A Selected Anthology (Porter and Dreier, 1973), were both published two years after I graduated from NU.

In short, NU graduates have made contributions to the discipline. The faculty too has distinguished itself: several presidents of the SSSP have come from NU (Bernard Beck, Ray Mack, John Kitsuse, and Howard S. Becker). Raymond Mack was also an unsuccessful candidate for ASA president but held other important positions in the association. Many of them continue to publish widely, and perhaps in greater quantity than their students. Allen Schnaiberg, Janet Abu-Lughod, John Walton, Scott Greer, Richard Berk, Remi Clignet, and Chalres Moskos have all published at least one book in the time I left NU. Some of them are no longer at NU. Academic mobility has taken its effect. (For some reason, a large number have gone to sunny California.)

Academic Socialization

David Reisman makes an important distinction between sociology and professional fields such as law, medicine, and nursing. In the latter, an early and intensive form of re-socialization takes place that is soon legitimized at the moment of certification. Such students are treated as adults and as (pre) professionals -- in other words as future lawyers, doctors, and nurses. I am sorry to say that this does not always happen in the social sciences; one is not always treated as a colleague or a professional, and worse, one may never really know when one has been fully accpeted into the "club". I know full professors who still feel insecure about their status as sociologists. No governing board, no rite de passage, not even one's dissertation committee can give one the peace of mind to say: "Yes, I am now a professional sociologist, acceptable to my colleagues and teachers".

This academic state of limbo can last for many years after the Ph.D. and causes a great deal of anxiety. Eventually, however, one accepts oneself as a professional but only after many long years. Part of the "umbilical cord" problem alluded to earlier is to finally see oneself, not as a student, but as an equal partner in the sociological enterprise. This problem may be even more acute for female sociologists because of the added dilemma of sex-role stereotyping.

How does one become socialized into a profession? The most common method is to serve an apprenticeship under one or several models and this is what happens in grad school. The search for a mentor is crucial, but what is really needed is to find one faculty "super-star" and two or three supporting "stars". The problem is the competition. Too often, the "superstar" is so popular he or she may be impossible to "catch".

Pierre van den Berghe points out in his humorous and quite useful book Academic Gamesmanship: How to Make a Ph.D. Pay (1970:33) that "...if (the superstar) has too many students, his ability to be of use to you will be diluted, and the competition within his coterie of clients will be intense. However, if you feel con-fident that you can outshine your competitors, then attach yourself to the star anyway".

But this may be difficult, as it was for me, be-cause the "superstar" I wanted (Howie Becker) had too many students. I finally chose a fine Ph.D. committee consisting of Janet Abu-Lughod, Allen Schnaiberg, and Richard Schwartz. Choosing a dissertation committee in such a highly charged atmosphere as van de Berghe described is a critical factor in post-graduate school success since their letters of recommendation are key elements in career advancement, especially for the first job. Usually after that, the young assistant professor is on one's own, but those letters from dissertation chairpersons are still important years later. One's career will be followed closely by the department for the rest of one's life. For good or ill, what one does reflects on one's teachers, negati-vely or positively.

Regarding sex discrimination in choosing the "superstars", there was none that I knew of at NU. The department was seen as quite liberal, even radical, and while the feminist movement had not yet reached its peak there or in the country, there were a good number of women among the grad students. (Out of 80 students in the sociology department between 1967-1968, 28 were women, or 35 percent.)

Both women and men had equal access to the "superstars"; it all depended on the right combination of talents, interests, and personality mesh. However, I am aware that a major concern of the feminist movement is the lack of adequate role models for women. That may have been a problem back then; there were few women teachers between 1967-1971 -- only three out of some twenty positions, or fifteen percent. But, by 1979, the number of women had jumped to eight out of 21 teachers or 38 percent. Affirmative action was on the move. From 1967-1971, there were no full women professors; today there are two in the department (Janet Abu-Lughod and Arlene Kaplan Daniels).

Regarding other minorites, in my graduate days, there was only one Black professor (Walter Wallace, now at Princeton); today, there are four of them, a jump from five to nearly 20 percent. As for Asian-Americans, there was only one (John Kitsuse) a dozen years ago, and after he left, there were none. While Jews are not considered a minority group in affirmative action, professors of Jewish background made up about 50 percent back in 1967-1971 and today that figure is roughly the same. In short, for Blacks and women there are many more role models than there were even a dozen years ago.

Political Tensions

These were years of great student and societal upheaval, and no description can fully describe the power of those times. NU sociology students were right in the center of the action. While politically, they were spread across the spectrum from conservative to liberal to revolutionary, most were on the left-to-liberal side of the fence. (This is not surprising for sociologists or their grad students, and is backed up by research by Ladd and Lipset, 1975: 93-124.)

There was a small but noticable contingent of students who came out of the military (Bob Carroll, Frank

Osanka) who were attracted to the military sociology specialists at NU and U. of C. -- Charles Moskos and Morris Janowitz. these included several army officers (including one major and a captain), West Point instructors, and a CIA specialist in counter-insurgency. Their support of the Vietnam War came under attack by the majority of students in the department.

Our department, it must be noted, was considered one of the most radical on campus, and such student leaders as Lee Weiner, one of the famous Chicago "Eight" who went on trial for demonstrations at the 1968 Democratic convention, were graduate students. Weiner had the sympathy and respect of several key and influential faculty members and was an enormously charismatic student. Even the faculty was in awe of him and his prodigious mind.

The Black students were also highly politicized, staging a sit-in on campus that received national coverage. One of the key spokesman at that sit-in, James Turner, was a highly respected grad student in the department. James Pitts, who was to return to NU as an assistant professor, was also quite active. Black demands were more readily accepted than those of white radicals, and out of the sit-in came a Black Studies program, more Black students and teachers, and a home on campus called FMO, For Members Only.

The women's movement, on the other hand, had not yet fully broken away from the male-dominated anti-war movement but this was soon realized and women have made many strides for equality since then. The local SDS (Students for a Democratic Society) were led by under-graduate students and they distrusted the graduate students to some degree because they felt they were too "moderate". I would use the term "level-headed" instead. SDS was led by a very idealistic yet impulsive and paranoid group of individuals. There were times when we graduate students tried (unsuccessfully) to stop them from committing acts of violence (i.e., attacking a ROTC building) even after they had gotten strong student support for their positions on the war and on ROTC. In that sense, SDS was often "suicidal" politically (a term that was also used then was "Custeristic"), and it was ultimately dis-credited in the eyes of most students.

On the academic level, the graduate students were active in educational reforms and policies. Having had sympathetic faculty members made that task easier. For example: great changes were made in what were called the "qualifying exams" -- the exams that one took to pass from stage to stage, from M.A. to Ph.D. for example. Instead of the traditional two six-hour doctoral qualifying examinations, we instituted a series of alternatives that still exist a decade later.

Students now had a choice of (a) the traditional sit-down exams; (b) the same exams but take-home; (c) a qualifying paper akin to a Master's Thesis; or (d) the innovative part -- a judgement on one's previously published material. Ironically, here was a radical demand that was first taken advantage of by one of those in the "conservative camp". The counter-insurgency expert from the CIA had edited a book on guerilla warfare and had written several important articles in the field and this made it possible for him to pass what the students called "Check-Point-Charlie" -- the set of procedures that enable one to go on and write the dissertation and thereby obtain the Ph.D. This "check-point" was considered to be the most difficult stage in graduate school. If successfully passed it almost assured one's getting a Ph.D.

The faculty was also responsive to new courses and innovative approaches to old courses -- especially those that reflected the latest political strife: a seminar on the Black revolutionary Frantz Fanon taught by Professor Remi Clignet; a seminar on revolutionary movements; a seminar on the sociology of art; and one on the art and science of teaching. I am most proud of the last course because I helped organize and direct it. (For other innovative approaches to teaching, see Porter, 1974).

As can easily be imagined, graduate school between 1967-1971 was a time of great stress. Graduate school is always tension-filled, but those years were especially tumultuous. One's personal philosophy and way of life come under seething attack. Long-cherished beliefs from home and neighborhood are vulnerable to the teachings of sophisticated and secular college professors.

For example, I had entered NU with a fairly secure set of religious and political beliefs concerning Judaism, Jews, and Israel, and I had also come from a very Orthodox Jewish background. All my beliefs came under intense criticism by secular leftists and liberals in the department over the issue of Zionism and Jewish rights. In response, my views changed or were modified. (See section on religious tensions). I had to find some golden mean between traditional Judaism and such modern ideologies as radicalism and socialism.

Out of my personal and political _angst_ would emerge a book called _Jewish Radicalism_ (Porter and Dreier, 1973) and a later evaluation (Dreier and Porter, 1975). It also led to my founding, along with a few other NU graduate students (none in sociology), the Jewish Student Movement in Chicago, one of the first in the country. Such a group would be an activist group in Jewish as well as anti-war and civil rights concerns. It would be critical of both the Jewish establishment in America and Israel and any Black, radical, or Third World group who espoused anti-Semitism or anti-Zionism. These political and intellectual efforts meshed to help me re-orient myself and is a process that continues to this very day. It is the continuous shifting, adapting, and accommodating of political and religious beliefs in order to fit new realities. The genesis of these tensions in my life emerged out of my 1967-1971 graduate days.

Those years vividly raised an old question in science -- the tension between the detached, objective scholar and the involved, subjective partisan. Is it our task to study society or to change it ... or both? I have opted for Marx's dictum -- to understand and to transform. In the end, many of us at NU tried to do both good scholarly work and good political work. My own way out of the dilemma was to demonstrate against ROTC in the morning and to write my dissertation about ROTC at night (Porter, 1971). I was a kind of "schizophrenic" participant observer. Looking back, perhaps _both_ the dissertation and the politics suffered. I had spread myself too thin. Still, to this day, I combine activism and scholarship and I let others decide what suffers. I no longer worry about this existential question.

In conclusion, I have several regrets about those years. First of all, we did not win all our battles for justice and equality. We had to leave a few things for future generations! But also, another thing stands out in my mind: my moral outrage against the war often stifled effective communication with people who disagreed with me. I now wish I could have had more

-41-

dialogue with the West Point officers and other military specialists, with the more conservative professors, school administrators, and students, and with the outside world. But we were acting out a huge pageant and like puppets, <u>deus ex machina</u>, we played out our elected roles with history.

Psychological Tensions

The conflicts of academic training can often lead to acute psychological stress, and this stress can lead to a variety of coping mechanisms. The stress of competition in graduate school can, for example, induce a wide variety of cheating, some of it done at a very unsophisticated level -- blatant plagiarism, prewritten papers and theses, or simply copying answers from someone else. I knew a student, who ripped an exam off my desk in order to copy the answers to an extremely difficult statistics test. In most ways, he was an honest student but for his desperate fear of mathematics. He passed the test and today he is a well-respected sociologist at a well-known university.

The pressures can also lead to more serious problems -- to what is commonly called "nervous breakdowns" but are really acute anxiety attacks. In many cases, the faculty and students were totally unaware of these "breakdowns" if the person managed, with great effort and pain, to turn in required assignments. The rationale is that if one can still "produce", if one can still work, that in itself can stave off the realization that one is "totally crazy".

One of the most cruel and least understood tragedies of graudate life is suicide, and it strikes every campus. The only case in our class was a divorced mother of three who had returned to school after long years at home raising children. She was also one of the few "flunkouts" in our class, having failed her Ph.D. qualifying exams and was told not to apply again. As a "consolation prize" she was given a terminal master's degree. During the last year or two of her short life, she engaged in a series of highly bizarre acts: she spied on a particular professor; she drove to his home, waited for him to come home to his family, and peeked into his windows. Sometimes, she waited for him all night long in her car and then followed him to school in the morning. She also suffered from acute pangs of paranoia wherein she thought everyone, including her friends, were in a conspiracy against her and she threatened to sue the department for being unfairly dismissed. She was told by the chairman of the sociology department to seek psychiatric treatment but to no avail. A year after my graduation in 1971, I learned of her suicide.

While there is little one can do for a person bent on destroying oneself and while there are often tell-tale signs along the way, most people are still shocked. Most of the faculty will not become involved unless the behavior is truly unusual or if it effects one's work. As Craig Eisendrath and Thomas Cottle (1972: 54) point out:

> With the exception of some extraordinary people, faculty find such matters out of line with their own stated careers of scholarly concerns, or they feel themselves unable to deal with what they conceive of as the students' "psychological" problems. Indeed, some will even maintain that whatever these troublesome problems may be, the students should buckle down and get to work.

Even though teachers are concerned with the mental health of their students, they find it awkward to get "involved" in these problems which they see as being outside their realm of competence, and they tend to resist efforts to make them more involved. As Eisendrath and Cottle point out:

> It is adult attention, among other things, that these young people seek, but the nature of many educational institutions prevents them from receiving it. (1972: 54-55)

Moreover, a school's health services can never compensate for a lack of human care on the part of faculty and administration, and for a system of education which fails to nurture the autonomy and competence which students lack when they enter. Most faculty fail to actively involve themselves with the mental health of their students and in doing so, they exacerbate the health of the very students they are there to help.

Perhaps, Eisendrath and Cottle are too hard on faculty. Most are concerned, more are aware of suicide and other psychological problems, and clinics have been set up to intervene. But in the late 60's it was a taboo subject. Still, it is an area that more faculty and students must be attuned to, and in any discussions of academic history or departments, it is common phenomenon.

Sexual Tensions

If death and mental illness are still "closet" subjects to some degree, sex has emerged out of the dark, and yet we know very little about the sexual problems of graduate students. I am concerned here not with the physical act but with the social relationship. Relationships among graduate students are analogous to sibling rivalry and therefore "incestuous". Each sibling is competing desperately for the approval of multiple father or mother figures. Furthermore, business and pleasure rarely mix and so I remember that most students sought out students in other departments or in other schools for sexual gratification.[3]

For single and divorced students there is the problem of time and energy needed to search out and find suitable partners. Often, that is why student-teacher or undergraduate-graduate student relations are so common: availability. There is also another reason that is only now coming to light. Teaching, as the late social thinker Paul Goodman has noted, has sexual overtones. A large pool of single men and women (students) and a powerful leader (the teacher) can set us a situation that can lead to sexual favors given or rejected. The teacher, even the graduate instructor, is a position to seek out attractive partners of the opposite (or even same) sex in exchange for higher grades or simply as a sign of dominance. Examples of blatant sexuality and sexual favors among students and teachers were so common that few considered them a problem if they were carried out with discretion. However, the feminist movement has exposed this practice, and many instructors will think twice about engaging in sex with a student today. Still, the practice continues and has ramifications beyond this short paper.

As for the impact of graduate training on marriage, again we need more research. While the common assumption is that graduate school puts a great strain on marriage (and it does) and leads to higher rates of divorce, one should also note, as I have, the number of marriages that survive graduate school and prevail. What accounts for this success? What are the stress factors? What can be done to help wives and husbands of graduate students through this <u>rite de passage</u>? It would behoove us to formulate humane policies and frameworks to deal with the issue.

Religious Tensions

This issue may seem irrelevant to some readers but it is important. Sociology continues to attract people from the religious life just as it has 80 or more years ago when large numbers of American sociologists were the sons of Protestant ministers. Could sociology be a secular substitute for the religious life? In any case, our department had a small but visible number of priests, nuns, seminarians, or simply people from an orthodox background, such as myself.

Being young and impressionistic, my religious beliefs were shaken at NU and there were few role models in the department who were both Jewish and proud of it. As I discussed earlier, this led to a painful re-orientation basically done on my own but with the help of the NU Hillel Foundation rabbi and several graduate students who shared a similar anguish. Just as Blacks, women, Asian-American, and other minorities need role models, so too do Jews. While half the department was Jewish, only a few were willing to discuss my interests in Israel and Judaism. The rest were assimilated Jews or had other, more important interests. Nevertheless, it was a painful process.

I have discussed my own socialization problems regarding religious tensions. There were others in the department -- nuns, priests, ministers -- with similar tensions. Coming under the stress of the secular university life, some left the clergy altogether or else found some compromise, perhaps a secular substitute for "people-healing" (i.e., social work, counseling). All of them had to modify their own religious attitudes and life styles, and usually religious tensions went hand-in-hand with political and psychological ennui. (For more on this tension, see Kotre, 1978, on the life of Father Andrew Greeley, sociologist and priest.)

Conclusions

On a recent visit to my <u>alma mater</u> (winter of 1975), one of my professors sadly remarked that so few

of the students in our class of 1971 were actually
doing sociology. He was frankly discouraged, while
other faculty members were angered at the waste of time
and trouble. Still others were simply resigned to the
fact. As one put it:

> All one need do is peruse the journals to
> note the absence of the Northwestern cohort
> members.... Faculty concern with this group
> (and not just the "rebels") centers on the
> inability of a large number of these people
> to engage in quality research, consultation,
> or teaching. Witness their presence in the
> job market year after year. (Anonymous
> letter by reviewer, March 1977)

This professor has no firm data to rely on and
neither do I, but a closer look at those who graduated
with me does show that a good many are involved in
sociology in one way or another. Many may have gone
into alternative life styles or careers, either temporarily or permanently, but the majority are involved
in either teaching sociology or "applying" it as social
workers, drug counselors, public health professionals,
and similar work. Given the present job scarcity of
academic positions, the number may not be at all dis-
couraging. Many are not writing in journals that this
professor cherishes or are not doing the "quality
reserach" he desires, but given the economic situation,
perhaps other skills should have been taught them so as
to better cope with the "job crunch" (see Morrissey and
Steadman, 1977).

Nevertheless, the 1967-1971 cohort is teaching at
fine schools; for example: Yale, Stanford, Wisconsin,
University of Washington, Amherst, University of
Hawaii, Boston College, Rutgers, McGill, Cornell, and
several others. Very few graduate students in any case
become renowned in their field and very few even
publish books, but NU graduates have published several
books; they have published articles in prestigious
journals like the American Sociological Review and
Social Problems; and some have even founded scholarly
journals (George Kourvetaris of the Journal of Military
and Political Sociology and Jack Nusan Porter of the
Journal of the History of Sociology; and several are
active in professional groups and as journal editorial
board members. I don't believe that their output has
been minor when compared to graduates of Chicago,
Harvard, or Columbia, but in any case, this is all con-

jecture. Until the NU sociology department conducts its own full-scale survey, we will never know for sure, one way or the other.

Still, the major question, the <u>leit</u> <u>motif</u> really of this article, is: to whom do you owe your life? to yourself or to your professors? Do professors have the right to mold their students into a model of their own making? Perhaps they do but should they be disappointed if that mold cracks and another persona emeges? There comes a time when professors too must break the "umbilical cord" with their students and accept alternative life styles to simply that of professional scholar. Graduate schools must today present <u>other</u> models, given the scarce number of jobs, and they <u>are</u> beginning to do just that today.

Here are some examples of what this 1967-1971 cohort has done:

<u>Item</u>: One student dropped out of training before completing his Ph.D. in order to become director of an Afro-American studies institute at a major university. Years later, he received his Ph.D. but from another college, and he is still director of that institute.

<u>Item</u>: One politically active student also did not complete his dissertation but went out to teach at a major East Coast university. He lost his job under administration pressure because of an article that appeared in a New York paper regarding his political views and activities. He is today a social worker in New York City and later completed his Ph.D. in sociology.

<u>Item</u>: Another student temporarily dropped out of school to become an organic food farmer on an island on the Northwest Coast. Yet, he too completed his dissertation and now teaches in a large public university.

<u>Item</u>: Another decided to become a medical doctor after dropping out with only his master's degree. He is now a physician.

<u>Item</u>: Another student lived in the Rocky Mountains and supported himself as a musician, but I've seen him recently at a sociology conference and he has returned to teaching and completing his studies.

<u>Item</u>: Another student has published a dozen books and over 150 articles and reviews in the general area

of ethnic studies but finds it difficult to find a full-time position because of the economic situation. He is listed in Who's Who in the East, American Men and Women of Science and American Authors, but it doesn't help. Still, he continues in sociology.

Item: One student joined the Montreal Symphony Orchestra.

Item: And, finally, another works in San Francisco for the recreation department and ended his NU studies after obtaining his master's degree. He does no more sociology.

The crucial question remains: to whom do you owe your life: to what use must you make of your education? Is graduate training a complete waste of time if one decides to do something else? These are not easy questions to answer. To continue this line of reasoning, if a Ph.D. in sociology took his skills and joined the staff of a political organization, a consumer group, a religious institution, or community project, and forsake teaching and research, what would his or her professors think? (In today's shrinking job market, they'd be happy he/she is not driving a cab!) But professors are demanding other things as well. Many want their students not only to do sociology (research and teaching), and this is a fair and reasonable demand, but to do the right kind of sociology.

What if a student did go into research but did it in a very different way -- a Marxist approach? a radically feminist approach? a Jewish approach? a new and vastly critical approach (of their own teacher's, no less)? What then? Alvin Gouldner answers it best: "There is no such thing as Black, white, feminist, Jewish, Christian, radical, sexist, or gay sociology, hard or soft sociology ... there is only good or bad sociology!" (Personal conversation with author, August 1975, Boston)

Yet, what is often overlooked is that the vast majority of my classmates are immersed in the sociological enterprise in one way or another. Many are in academia, too, or trying to get back in. They are teaching. They are acting as consultants. They are lecturing to community groups. A few are even doing research and trying to get it published. There may not be enough being published to please some of my professors, but there may be powerful reasons besides motivation behind that -- lack of research money, lack of time, and difficulty getting into those prestigious journals that their professors are reading.

Epilogue

It has been impossible to summarize in a few pages four of the most tumultuous and important years of my life. Whenever I look back at those year, I feel a tinge of pity for today's students. They are too young to have taken part in the 1960's -- Vietnam, the demonstrations, Kent State University, Jackson State College, ROTC protests, hippies; these are just another chapter in history books. Only the faculty remembers and those of us who lived through those powerful years. As one Boston student leader put it:

> The masses aren't marching this year. The masses are in the library. They take school work soooo seriously .... Everybody's just fuckin' blah. I can't offer any original explanation except, at Harvard, everyone's studying. Everyone wants to go to grad school. Everyone wants to be doctors or lawyers. Everyone wants to make lots of money. (Harvard Crimson, Editor, Jim Cramer, as quoted in Span, 1976:10)

These same views were echoed by a Northeastern University (Boston) student president:

> Deep down, the fact is that a lot of kids wish they were going to college in the 1960's when students got together more often and were active. (Quoted in Span, 1976:10)

History, however, moves in cycles. The 1970's student lived through a '50's apathetic concern for security, but the 1980's has brought back student protest over the draft, Iran, the economy. Living through the 1960's was not easy. It reminds me of the old Chinese curse: "May you live in interesting times." We did indeed live through interesting times, and as our class enters early middle age, we wouldn't replace those years for anything.

1976

<u>Notes</u>

This paper was first presented at the American Sociological Association Professional Workshop on "Survival in Graduate School", August 1976, New York City. I have kept anonymous names of students and teachers where such disclosure would prove to be embarrassing or rude. This paper was not meant to appeal to "prurient interests" but to raise issues that are often concealed. My apologies to those who feel otherwise.

1. Several Chicago students did tell me how they envied the close-knit relationship among faculty, staff, and students. Teachers often threw parties for students and students invited teachers to their parties and even secretaries hosted parties for everyone. If I seem to emphasize this social side of academic life, it is because it is an important socializing element in graduate school. Such years are filled with pressure and any way to relive the pressure and enhance more open and warm relations should be welcome. In other words, what the U. of C. students were saying was that even though they may have been going to a slightly more prestigious school, they nevertheless felt deprived of faculty understanding, and <u>that</u> counted higher than any added prestige.

2. Even these students have students now. For example, I have had two students who have gone into sociology, and one of them, Barry Glassner, has gone on to make quite a name for himself at a very young age. In short, the cycle continues.

3. The sexual issues are sensitive enough without even mentioning homosexual concerns. That was even more of a taboo subject back then.

References

Dreier, Peter and Jack Nusan Porter, "Jewish Radicalism in Transition" Society (Transaction), Vol. 12, No. 2, Jan.-Feb. 1975.

Eisendrath, Craig R. and Thomas J. Cottle, Out of Discontent: Visions of the Contemporary University, Boston: Schenkman Publishing Company, 1972.

Kotre, John N., The Best of Times, the Worst of Times: Andrew Greeley and American Catholicism, 1950-1975, Chicago: Nelson-Hall, 1978.

Ladd, Everett Carll and Seymour Martin Lipset, The Divided Academy: Professors and Politics, New York: McGraw-Hill, 1975.

Morrissey, Joseph P. and Henry J. Steadman, "Practice and Perish? Some Overlooked Career Contingencies for Sociologists in Non-Academic Settings", The American Sociologist, Vol. 12, No. 4, Nov. 1977, 154-162.

Porter, Jack Nusan, Student Protest, University Decision-Making, and the Technocratic Society: The Case of ROTC, Dept. of Sociology, Evanston, Illinois: Northwestern University, 1971. Dissertation also available from University Micro-films. A shorter version was published by Adams Press, Chicago in 1973.

Porter, Jack Nusan, "A New Course Proposal: Sociology in Practice", ASA Footnotes, Vol. 2, No. 6, August 1974, 6-7.

Porter, Jack Nusan and Peter Dreier, Jewish Radicalism: A Selected Anthology, New York: Grove Press, 1973.

Span, Paula, "We Search for the New Campus Leaders", The Boston Phoenix (Special Education Section), April 6, 1976, 8-10.

Van den Berghe, Pierre, Academic Gamesmanship: How to Make a Ph.D. Pay, New York: Abelard-Schuman (an Intext Book), 1970.

THE DEATH OF A FATHER

The phone call came on a Thursday night. My mother was crying on the phone for the first time. She could hardly say the words: "He's not talking anymore. He sits in the chair but he doesn't talk."

My father had been struggling with the pain for nearly four years, first cancer of the prostrate, later cancer of the bone marrow. His doctors were angry at themselves. Not because they couldn't save his life but because they couldn't stop his pain. The cancer had metasticized into crevices of the body that drugs could not reach. He was on constant morphine.

* * * *

My father had been a fairly healthy man, working as he did with iron and steel in his small scrap-metal business. He had the heart of a 40-year old man. During World War II, he was one of the few Jewish commanders of a partisan brigade. He had been honored with a medal by the Russian government for valor. After he came to America in 1946, he worked in a shoe factory in Milwaukee to support his wife and two young sons, my brother Shlomo and me. He finally quit factory life because his boss insisted that he work on the Sabbath, and my father, an Orthodox Jew, could not do that. So, he went into partnership with a German Jew, Sigmund Singer, and after a few years and many quarrels, started his own business. He worked very hard breaking steel, taking apart furnaces, picking up lathe turnings, and selling them to richer men who owned their own scrap iron and waste yards. They in turn would sell it to steel mills in America, Japan, and Germany.

My father had lost two daughters and 25 members of his family to the Nazis, and perhaps work was an anodyne; and a religion too. My father never lost his faith in God.

* * * *

I tried to carry on with my life after the call -- teaching, correcting exams, writing, the usual duties of a college teacher, but I knew I would be going to Milwaukee very soon to see my father. My brother and his wife had already flown in from California, where he

is a "rebbe" at a yeshiva in Santa Clara; and my sister
and her husband had arrived from Minneapolis. The
waiting began. As I drove to the university, I could
not stop crying. I had to pull the car over to the
side more than once because I could not see the road.

After two worrisome days, the call finally came
last Saturday night. It was my sister. "You better
come. It doesn't have to be tonight, but take the
earliest plane tomorrow."

Sunday morning, my wife drove me to the airport
and I left Boston on the first flight. A friend picked
me up, and after dropping my luggage at the house, I
walked to St. Joseph's Hospital, located only a block
from my parents' home.

My father was on the cancer ward. He was propped
up in bed, oxygen tubes in his nose. He recognized me
and we embraced. His face was the same except for dark
shadows around his eyes. His cheeks were still a bit
pink. Every word he spoke was difficult. My mother,
sister, and brother, plus a few close friends were
there. All of us know what was happening. We tried to
be brave.

During the day and into the night, we kept vigil.
Friends and relatives came and went. My brother
constantly chanted the Tehilim, Psalms.

The doctor told me that Tateh (Dad in Yiddish) had
contracted pneumonia because his defense against infec-
tions had been shattered by the cancer. It was a
matter of days now. My response was surprisingly
angry: "Your job is over, doctor. Now let God do what
He can." He nodded his head in agreement and left.

The next twenty-four hours were unbelievable. We
sat around the bed, telling my father news of our
lives. We sang some songs in Yiddish, a few Sabbath
songs. We could see that he was drifting into another
realm. He spoke in Russian, a language he rarely used
around us. He shouted Choroshoy, "Its's o.k.," in
Russian. He was dreaming of his youth, of his days in
the partisans. Perhaps, he was comforting us
--Choroshoy!

The day before, on Shabbat, when our rabbi, Reb
Michel Twerski, came to visit him, my father sang with
him, and as Rabbi Twerski left and said good-bye, my

father corrected him and said, "Not good-bye, I'll see you tomorrow."

Sunday evening my brother gave my father a new name, _Rephual_. His name was Israel, but according to Jewish custom, when a person is grievously ill he receives a Kabbalistic name to confuse the angel of death. If he or she survives, they keep that name --_Rephual_, ("God will heal"), _Chayyim_, or _Chaya_ for the rest of their life. If they lapse into another serious illness, they receive another name, and another. . . The names mean "Health," "Life". My brother told me of a man who has gone through four or five names and is still alive.

My father gave all of us his last blessings. To me, he said: "_Mach a leben, Yankele. Es is shver tzu machen a leben in America._" ("Make a living, Jackie. It's hard to make a living here.") To my mother, he said: "It's enough for you, Momma. Be strong. It will soon be over."

Each minute in that hospital room seemed like eternity. Night came. We didn't know what else to do except pray and sing. My brother took out the holy _siddur_ of Rabbi Jacob Emden, a 16th century German Kabbalist and scholar. The hospital was quiet. We were alone with my father when a most miraculous event occurred.

As my brother Shlomo read from the text, I could almost feel the room fill up with angels. I could hear their flapping wings. My father's soul was in the room and was speeding toward heaven.

> On your right flies the angel Raphael; and on your left, the angel Gabriel. The _Keter_ (crown) is at your head and the _malchut_ (kingdom) at your feet. Angel wings protect and cover your chest and angel wings cover your feet. You are flying toward heaven carried by angels.

My brother prayed and then translated the Hebrew into Yiddish. We cried. We prayed. We were astounded. We could hear our father saying goodbye. The soul was winging toward the heavens, toward the world to come, to _Gan Eden_ or to Gehinnom, to heaven or hell, but we knew it was heaven. With tears in my eyes, I asked Shlomo: "He's going to heaven?"

"No question about it, Jack. He's going straight
to heaven."

* * * *

I thought only Christians had an afterlife and
that Jews did not. Heaven was always something quite
vague, something one never discussed in Hebrew or
Sunday school. Perhaps the rabbis were trying to tell
us something with their reticence. Concentrate on <u>this</u>
life, don't concern yourself with the world to come.
Geoffrey Gorer has called it the "pornography of
death"; that is, death has replaced sex as the last
obscenity to be kept from the eyes of children and
adults. Yet, in Judaism it is not simply fear of death
but the assumption that to dwell upon death or the
afterlife could lead to madness. Thus, <u>Kabbalah</u>, which
does deal with these issues, could only be studied by
mature, married individuals, steeped in Talmud and
Torah. Before you can run you must first learn to
crawl and then to walk. The same with <u>Kabbalah</u>. You
must first learn the basics.

I am essentially a secular Jew. I live a life
based on reason. Never would I have thought that I
would so fervently believe in angels or heaven and
hell. My brother and I talked about this, at times in
earshot of my father. He explained to me that Judaism
has a complex map of the afterlife and that Christians
took their system from the Jews. Very evil people go
to hell; a small number are in limbo; but most people
will reside (their souls will reside) at various
<u>madregot</u> (steps or stages) of heaven. <u>Tateh</u> would be
at a fairly high level because he was a righteous man,
and he would move up the <u>madregot</u> as time went by. At
the very highest levels are the souls of Abraham,
Isaac, and Jacob, Moses, Solomon, David, and all the
great prophets and rabbis of ancient times. To be
invited to sit at their table is the greatest of
heavenly delights.

I was also intrigued by another thing my brother
said. How can a soul move up in heaven after the person dies? The individual is no longer able to carry
out <u>mitzvot</u> or acts of righteousness. How then can he
or she be lifted up still higher? The answer is unu-
sually innovative. It is the family and friends of the
deceased who, through good deeds and acts of kindness,
can lift their beloved higher and higher throughout
eternity. The poignancy of this idea overwhelms me at
times.

* * * *

Sunday night the doctors informed us that <u>Tateh</u> was entering irreversible shock. He would live only as long as his powerful heart would hold out, twelve hours, a day, perhaps two days.

We prayed even more. We sang. We talked with Dad. Perhaps he heard us. I'd like to think that he did.

We took turns with the vigil. Friends came. Some were so distraught they had to leave. We waited. My brother slept in the hospital all night. I went home, knowing that in the morning my father might be dead.

I returned to his room in the morning -- praying, hoping. I went home for lunch. At 12:15 p.m., Monday, March 19, my sister Bella called: "Jack, it's over."

I would not believe it. I didn't hear it. I would continue life as usual. I calmly finished my soup, trying to ignore the phone conversation. Then, I quickly walked to the hospital. When I entered the ward, I knew it was over when I saw the nurses crying. My father had also touched them deeply.

I walked into the room. My mother was weeping over his body, and she wailed: "You see. This is what your <u>Tateh</u> has now become." I went to the bed and embraced by father for the last time, and taking his strong and beautiful hand I said: "Good-bye, <u>Tateh</u>. You were the best." I broke into tears and just <u>looked</u> at him, holding his hand for a long time, until it got colder and colder.

The nurses, who had been trained in a special kind of primary care, comforted my mother, giving her a sedative and putting warm blankets around her. She was shivering uncontrollably and the nurses who knew of her heart condition were worried. I embraced a sad and dejected Dr. Hurwitz, my father's physician. He was totally leveled. To him, death was a monumental symbol of his failure as a healer.

"Be comforted that he is out of his pain, Jack." He was a caring man and he needed <u>my</u> comfort at that moment.

Our rabbi, Reb Michel Twerski, arrived within minutes. Immediately, a new phase began -- the mourning process, and this too was ensconced in four thousand years of law and tradition. The first ritual was that of Keriah, the rending of clothes. Reb Michel went up to my brother and me, made a small cut in our shirt or jacket with a pocket knife and we tore it down the size of our fist. We would wear these mourning clothes for the next seven days.

* * * *

I never knew how much work would follow a death. The chevra kadisha (literally "holy society" -- a Jewish burial society) arrived soon after the rabbi. They had been well trained and knew exactly what to do. My family and I could go home to begin the shiva, the seven days of mourning.

My father's body would be watched by a guard (a shomer in Hebrew) from the moment of his death to his burial, which would take place within 24 hours. I was not allowed to observe it, but my father was taken to the funeral home (it could have easily been the synagogue as well) where the tahara would be performed. The tahara is the ritual washing and dressing of the body in preparation for the afterlife. A son should not take part unless there is no one else who can do it.

A few years ago, in 1975, I had the honor of aiding in the tahara of the great Rabbi Jacob Twerski of Milwaukee, Reb Michel's father. So, I will describe that rather than my father's tahara. After immersing themselves in the mikveh or ritual bath, the men entered the synagogue where Rabbi Jacob lay in state and carefully washing the entire body in the proscribed manner. As Maurice Lamm notes in his book The Jewish Way in Death and Mourning, the tahara is not only the preparation of the body but the reciting of the proper prayers asking God for forgiveness for any sins the deceased may have committed and praying that the All-Merciful should grant him/her eternal peace.

Men do the tahara on men and women on women. After the body is washed, it is clothed in a perfectly clean, perfectly white shroud. Holy soil from Israel is placed on the eyes and upon the forehead. No autopsies or cremations are allowed unless under extreme circumstances such as a plague. The body is placed in a simple wooden casket and again guarded by the shomer until the funeral begins.

* * * *

My brother said that one phone call is sufficient to spread the news. "Bad news travels fast. Each person will call another." However, it isn't that simple in a complex society. Relatives in other states had to be called, telegrams to Israel sent, the newspapers had to be informed so that the death notice could be inserted. And the mourning had to continue. Mourners, according to Jewish law, should really not do this work. In fact, they should do nothing else except mourn during the seven days of the shiva.

Nevertheless, I had the onerous task of calling my father's business clients and customers, of writing his obituary, and of taking care of other minor details. My brother concentrated on the funeral arrangements. This is not the proper place to lament the rising costs of funerals and plots. But according to Jewish law, a traditional funeral must not be ostentatious. One must use a wooden casket and a minimum of flowers. Still, even with a simple casket and funeral, it cost my mother about $2,000 (with $750 going for the cemetary plots).

The funeral was set for three o'clock the next day, Tuesday. Since we children were already in Milwaukee, we had only to wait for someone from my Uncle Boris' family in Los Angeles, someone from my Aunt Betty's family in Chicago to come, and for my wife to arrive from Boston. They arrived in plenty of time.

Almost immediately upon hearing of my father's death, people sent baskets of fruit and telegrams and friends started arriving. It was wonderful to have the support of so many relatives and friends at this hour.

We sat on low chairs or on the floor of the house; the mirrors were covered; we wore slippers; we could not put on make-up, shave, or comb our hair for that week. The door was open. Visitors entered and quietly waited for us to greet them. The mourners could either remain silent or initiate conversation. When visitors left they did not say good-bye but repeated the words, "May you be comforted among the mourners of Jerusalem and Zion."

* * * *

The limousine picked us up at 2:30 p.m. to take us to the funeral home. It was a bit unreal. I thought these things happen to other people. We were giddy in the car, awed by the uniqueness of it. Such a fancy automobile.

We were ushered into the side room of the funeral home. I could see the beautiful pine-box casket, the candles, the crowd coming in. People queued up to greet us. Small trays of aspirin, smelling salts, and kleenex were on the tables to our side. The crowd was large, nearly 300 people. My father was loved and admired by many people, Jews and non-Jews, blacks and whites, young and old.

The survivors of the Holocaust, old friends, sat with us in the special ante-room reserved for the family. These survivors substituted for the sisters and brothers, cousins and nephews lost in the war.

Several rabbis requested to speak. We chose four, but easily a half-dozen would have gladly eulogized my father. My brother and I would speak after them -- giving our own personal thoughts.

I remember only a few sections from each speech. Reb Michel Twerski spoke eloquently of my father's years in the Russian partisan movement and his devotion to his family and the <u>shul</u>. His opening lines were chilling: "Irving Porter, an old fighter, has lost his first battle."

The next speaker was Rabbi David Shapiro who gave a very deep and very poetic interpretation of my father's life, comparing his home with the building of the Jewish Temple in Jerusalem.

Finally, Rabbi Isaac Lerer came up and read a beautiful poem that he had composed on the spot in honor of my father. Then, Rabbi Feldman spoke. All the eulogies were very moving.

Then, I walked forward, saluting my father as I walked by him. I had written the speech last night and that morning a reporter from the <u>Milwaukee Sentinel</u> had come over to do a story on my father and took a copy of the speech with him. Here are portions of it:

My father was an ambitious man. Yes, he was very ambitious, but not for fame, money, or power. His ambition was to help support his family and to help others. His home was

always open to any person .... He was basically a happy, lively man, and this, despite
the Nazi hell he had gone through. In fact,
he was often amused and sometimes saddened by
his American relatives who had all sorts of
material comforts yet were depressed. He
could never understand that. His advice was
always: "Zei labedik, yidden!" ("Be lively,
Jews!").... I often interviewed him on his
role during the Holocaust, and he left me
with an important legacy: a Jew can send no
one in his place. When the time came for him
to take revenge, nekumah, he left his family
and joined the partisans. Not to take
another's life, but to regain his dignity and
the dignity of his family .... His role made
a deep and lasting impression on me -- to
fight for Jewish rights throughout the world
.... He is gone, but our memories live on in
his essential goodness, his singing, his
dancing at weddings and parties .... He battled the cancer like he battled the Nazis --
an old partisan, a fighter till the end. He
was even more -- a man blessed with chen,
grace, a righteous man, even a lamed vovnik
.... We will never forget you or what you
did .... Goodbye, Tateh. I salute you, you
old partisan.

* * * *

The funeral was a blur, a dream. We arrived. The
body was placed into the ground. The prayers were
said. The Kaddish. The casket hit bottom. Then, all
the men took the shovel and threw earth on the casket.
When the grave was completely filled everyone left. It
was suddenly over. My wife, Miriam, told me of an
ancient Sephardic custom. Take a pebble, throw it over
your shoulder, and don't look back.

Every morning and evening, men came to my mother's
house and with a minyan (a group of ten men), my
brother and I said kaddish for my father.

We carried out the shiva through more tragedy. A
few weeks after my father's death, his brother Boris
died in Los Angeles, and a week or so later, my
mother's cousin, a women only sixty, died in Florida.

Our friends buoyed us up. One of the most
thoughtful cards we received said the following:

"Please accept our sincere sympathies on the death of your father and father-in-law, Irving Porter. Losing a parent is a very hard thing to deal with. Doubts, guilt, sorrow, grief, and regrets are all part of the mourning process. There is no magic way to get through this painful time. But somehow, sometimes it helps to know that you have friends who care. Jack, we are your friends and we care. Love, John and Laurie."

My very wise father-in-law, Mr. Joseph Almuly, talked to me about death after the shiva. A man in his early eighties, he quoted Cicero to me:

Why should we be afraid of death? If death is the link with past relatives and friends, then it is a wonderful thing, is it not? But if death is nothing, then why should we be afraid of nothing? In any case, no one has ever come back to tell us if it is nothing or if it is indeed the reunification with one's family....

I don't know about an afterlife, but I do know that there was a beginning before my birth and that my death is not an end .... That is the truth of the matter. All that I know is that life is very precious, very short, and very complicated.

1979

SAY SHALOM TO ONE WHO FOUGHT DEARLY AND GAVE FREELY

By William Janz

His shirt torn as a sign of mourning, Jack Porter talked about his father. Tuesday was the day of the funeral.

During World War II, his father, Irving Porter, lived "by the gun and by the bomb," as a friend said. The Nazis murdered 25 members of his family one night.

It was in 1942 in the Ukraine that Porter, a Jew, left his family and went into the woods to kill Germans.

"He felt guilty about leaving his family," said Jack Porter, 34, the eldest son. "He had to make a choice -- leave his family and fight or stay with his family. They talk about Jews dying passively. Whole families at one time. Some people look at it as cowardice. Was it cowardice to stay with your family?

"It wasn't easy to run away and fight, but that's what my father did. You live with that choice the rest of your life."

His father never forgot the day.

"'I ran away on a Wednesday,' my father told me. 'On Friday night the Germans took my family,' he said."

"Two daughters," Porter said. "His mother and father. All his sisters. His grandparents. Nephews and nieces. They were all executed in one night."

He paused.

"The SS would move in and take the Jewish families out," he said. "There were no concentration camps for these people. A ditch. They were lined up, shot down, lime poured over them. Then the SS moved on to the next town."

And the next ditch.

Irving Porter had one rifle and 150 bullets. He didn't have that many bullets for long.

"He was forced into killing people and he didn't like it," his son said. "He was forced into killing Nazis. He took _nekumah_ against them."

Revenge.

Porter joined a group of 50 partisans who had two rifles. But these people would have fought with shovels and rakes. When they had only one gun, they used that to get another.

In the midst of this terrible war, Porter discovered a miracle. The miracle was his wife, who should have been dead.

On the way to her grave, Faye Porter escaped and hid in a barn. Otherwise there would have been 26 dead that Friday in 1942.

During more than two years of fighting in the Ukraine, Porter became a senior assistant commander in the Kruk division, headed by a Ukrainian partisan with that name.

Porter and his companions slept during the day and at night blew up railroad tracks and police stations manned by Germans. If they had to, they would have thrown rocks.

When the enemy finally pulled out in 1944, then it was the partisans who began knocking on doors.

"My father said the partisans would go to the homes of collaborators, have quick trials and shoot them. Once, he said, he went to the house of a collaborator and he was told to shoot the man. He couldn't kill the man, he said. 'In battle, yes, I could,' he said. 'I can't face to face.' A friend killed the collaborator."

It was about this time that Jack Porter was born. He was what they called a partisan baby. The Porters had lost their two children and, like many Jews, they were quickly starting new families.

The Jews had lost so many that those who remained "had children as quickly as possible to try to replace all those who were killed," said the son who was born in the Ukraine, a replacement for one of the many who had died there.

As he talked about his father, Porter had two
pages of a eulogy in front of him. Some sentences on
the paper were crossed out; some words were added. His
father was a special person and these words he would
say at the funeral had to be special words:

"My father used to say, and it was quite true,
that some people lost their faith in God during World
War II. They saw so much death, they couldn't believe
in God.

"But my father told me he saw many miracles during
the war. Bullets would be flying all around him, once
even through his hat, but a bullet never touched him.
He was an Orthodox Jew who never lost his faith in
God."

Rabbi Isaac N. Lerer, a longtime friend of Irving
Porter, said, "He was an amazing individual. I was
overwhelmed with the stories of his life and we sat and
talked for hours. Here he lost his first two children
and his whole family and he had to live by the gun and
by the bomb and to fight for his life. And he came out
of it with a new spirit.

"The way they lived in the forest, welcoming
anyone into their group, sharing what they had. Here,
too, in Milwaukee, his home was always open to any
stranger. There was always a meal and people stayed
with him."

Porter who was known as Israel Puchtik in the
Ukraine, used forged passports to get to Austria after
the war. Then he moved to the United States and became
a scrap metal dealer in Milwaukee. After all his
fighting, he found a home where knocks on the door
weren't something feared.

In the eulogy, his son said, "He was a tzaddik --a
lamed vov-nik."

He was, according to his son, a righteous man, one
of the 36. There is a legend in Jewish history that in
every generation there are 36 people who do good,
battle evil and are never known.

His voice filled with emotion, tears coming to his
eyes, Jack Porter said, "He was a lamed vov-nik."

After wiping away the tears, Porter said, "My
father and mother opened their home and hearts to

everyone ... friends and strangers, to anyone who needed a place for the night.

"And I remember my father saying, 'We must stand up and stop killing people. Stop killing people everywhere.' That's what he said. He never thought of himself as a hero. The partisans never did that. I once met a partisan and he said, 'Don't call me a hero. I had a gun and I had to do what I did.'"

With one rifle and 150 bullets, his father did what he had to do, too. And when his bullets were gone, he found more.

On Monday, at the age of 73, an old partisan from the Ukraine, a man who loved Milwaukee, died in St. Joseph's Hospital, less than a block from his home.

"He battled cancer as bravely as he battled the Nazis," his son said in the eulogy. "He was an old partisan. A fighter 'til the end."

With great respect and on behalf of his mother, his brother, Rabbi Solomon, and his sister, Bella, who make up the family that emerged after that Friday night 37 years ago, Jack Porter said to his father, "Goodbye, Tateh. You were the best."

1979

NOT TO GO LIKE AN ANIMAL

By Barbara Fein

The year was 1942; the place, the town of Manie-wicze, near Kovel, state of Volynhia, in the Ukraine. Israel Puchtik knew he had little time. He threw away his jacket with the yellow piece of cloth that marked him as a Jew. He tucked his pants into his boots, picked up a pail, and passed by the guards as a farmer -- miraculously escaping into the woods.

That was Wednesday. On Friday night, the Germans came. They killed Israel Puchtik's two daughters, his mother, his father, his sisters, his grandparents -- 25 members of his family in all.

The story of Israel Puchtik is much like that of the 25,000 other Jewish partisans who were driven to fight back during World War II. But unlike two-thirds of them, he survived to tell his tale.

His name has been changed to Irving Porter; his address, to 2912 N. 50 Street, Milwaukee. But his memories of two and one-half years of resistance cannot go away ....

As Puchtik tells it, the situation in the Ukraine during the war was different than that in Germany. Here there was no Dachau, no Auschwitz, no Treblinka. Jews were not taken to concentration camps, but direct-ly to their graves -- large pits dug by Gentiles from neighboring towns.

"Nobody cared anything about the Jews," Puchtik said. "Hitler talked over the radio and said that Jews and dogs were the same thing. He told the people to treat the Jews like dogs."

The Germans, working together with the Ukranian police, first came to Maniewicze -- a town of about 2,500 -- in 1941. They killed 375 of the town's men, who thought they were being taken by trucks to work. Only those men who were hiding survived.

In mid-1942, the Germans came again to Maniewicze -- this time pushing women and children as well as men into the streets and driving them to their graves. Since most of the town's men had already been killed, they met with little resistance.

"They drove the Jews in the night -- on Friday night. They knew the families were together then and they would surprise them," Puchtik said. "They would kill the Jews, then have an orchestra and a big party. When they finished a job, they'd go on to the next little town."

* * * *

At this point, Puchtik had made up his mind that he was not going to "go like an animal." He wanted to take revenge. He would run away, even though it meant leaving his wife and family.

"I felt guilty. I knew my family would be killed but I ran away. I went on a Wednesday. On Friday night the Germans came," he said.

Puchtik escaped into the woods where he hid for a couple of weeks before going to the home of a Gentile friend -- one of the few Gentiles in the Ukraine willing to help a Jew. The man gave Puchtik a rifle and 150 bullets.

Puchtik and another young Jew who had escaped then lay down in the woods and shot at Germans as they passed by. They had heard there were groups of Jews working with the Russian partisans (Gentile Communists who were also being persecuted by the Germans) and they hoped to meet up with them.

They soon found a group of about 50 persons who had just two rifles among them. Within three months that group grew until it included 200 "fighters" (about 180 Jews and 20 Russians), 200 more men who guarded the others, and between 500 and 600 women and children.

One of those women was Puchtik's wife.

"When I was with the partisans, I asked all the farmers we saw about my family. They knew all the names of the Jews who were in the area," Puchtik said.

"One said that my sister's husband was hiding nearby. I went there and I didn't see a tall man who was my brother-in-law, but a little man who weighed 60 pounds," he said.

That little "man" turned out to be Puchtik's wife, who had jumped off a truck on the way to the graves and hid in a box in a barn without being discovered.

* * * *

Puchtik's partisan group became known as the "Kruk
Division." Its leader was Ukranian nationalist Nikolai
Kaniszczuk (Kruk); Puchtik (called Zalonka in the
underground) was its senior assistant commander.

Why was the leader of the group not a Jew?
According to Puchtik, the Jews were "business people,
townspeople" and had little tradition of hunting or
fighting. The Gentiles, on the other hand, knew the
woods.

"No one helped the Jewish partisans," Puchtik
said. "In groups where there were mostly Russians, the
Russian Army gave them support. The Free Poles gave
the Polish partisans support. But no one came to the
aid of the Jewish partisans."

That included other partisan groups. One day a
captain from a Russian partisan group about 20 miles
away was sent over to the Kruk Division. He had "done
something wrong" and his "punishment" was to be sent
over to the Jews.

That captain -- who was later found out to be a
Jew in disguise -- told the Kruk Division that when the
Germans invaded in 1941 they had left behind them huge
artillery shells, which the captain had buried nearby.
The shells weighed as much as 100 pounds and were
filled with gunpowder.

Puchtik and about 20 other men were taught to take
the shells apart so they were no longer dangerous.
They put them in large barrels of water, lit fires
under the barrels, and heated the powder in the shells
to a liquid state.

"We put this liquid under mines we made," Puchtik
said. "There was not too much face-to-face contact.
We would go out into the night with five or six people
and blow up water pumps, train tracks, and police
stations.

* * * *

This, then, was how Puchtik lived from mid-1942
until the Germans completely retreated from the Ukraine
at the end of 1944. All day long he would lay quietly
in the woods; at night, he would set and blow up mines.

The partisans got food from the Ukranian farmers, whom they threatened to shoot if they weren't given it "in good will."

Puchtik was 38 years old in December 1944, when his first son, Jack, was born. He decided that year that he was "too old" to wait to have another child.

"We were in a city by then but the Germans were still bombing the cities every day," he said. "So at night when my wife was pregnant we were going 10 miles out from the city and laying down, coming back in the morning."

After the war ended in 1945, Puchtik went to work for the Russians. They gave him a medal for the work he had done in the woods. But he wanted to go to Palestine.

Puchtik obtained forged passports from the underground Haganah and began the roundabout journey to reach the land, which was surrounded by the British blockade at the time. Puchtik, his wife, and small child got as far as Austria (the journey from Poland to Austria by train had taken a month), when they decided to come to America instead.

"We were in an American displaced persons camp in Austria when an American captain came over to me and started talking in Russian," Puchtik said. "He asked me if I had relatives in America -- I told him I had a brother, Morris Porter, in Chicago."

The American had someone who was going to New York put a picture of Puchtik in the Yiddish newspaper, The Daily Forward. Through the picture, his brother Morris contacted Puchtik and brought him to America.

* * * *

Israel Puchtik -- now Irving Porter -- has been in Milwaukee since 1946. His brother had to convince him not to make the difficult journey to Palestine, promising that if he didn't like America he would send him there later.

"I have not been to Israel, but my wife is there visiting now," Putchik said. "When for so many years we were sick and tired and we finally settled here, we stayed.

"I am happy here. I make a nice living. When our kids are married we will go to Israel," he said.

Through all of his experiences Israel Puchtik has remained a strict Orthodox Jew. When he found that the factories in America "chased" him "out" because he wouldn't work on Saturdays, he became a junk peddler instead.

"When today a man is 45 years old, he was in his teens in the 1940s. He saw with his own eyes his parents praying day and night -- but some got no help from God. He has a reason not to believe any more," Puchtik said.

"But I was 35 or 36 in the 1940s," he said, "and I have reason not to give up my belief. I saw miracles happen. Ninety-nine per cent of the time my life was on one hair. I have bullet holes all over my shirts and hats -- but my body was not touched."

Perhaps the harshest lesson taught to Israel Puchtik was that "a Jew can send no one to take his place." He learned that "no one except a Jew" really cares about Jews.

"I blame the Communists, America, everyone for what happened," he said. "Why do people have to kill? The trouble is that when you have a little hole you can patch it up, but you can't when it gets bigger."

"It started with the Jews," he said. "People didn't care. The whole world was dancing. After Hitler finished, the world found it had other Hitlers. Every nation that kills people is a Hitler. Even America is not without guilt."

1972

II. CONFRONTING THE HOLOCAUST

JEWISH WOMEN IN THE RESISTANCE

Jewish women during World War II played an important part in all phases of the anti-Nazi resistance: in the forests, in the ghettos, in the concentration camps, and in the illegal underground. Wherever there was Jewish resistance, there were courageous Jewish women -- some, very young girls -- who played a crucial role in every aspect of the resistance, often performing duties that men were incapable of handling. They served as couriers, saboteurs, underground ghetto fighters, death camp revolutionaries, spies, assassins and the famous "mothers of the ghettos" -- leaders who by their courage sustained the morale of those imprisoned, inspiring continued resistance.

Among the most well-known of these women of valor were Hannah Senesh, the young Haganah parachutist from Palestine; Rosa Robota and Mala Zimetbaum, active in the uprisings in the "planet of hell" known as Auschwitz; and Tzivia Lubetkin, a leader of the Warsaw Ghetto Uprising together with her husband Antek Zuckerman -- who, until her death at 64 in July, lived on Kibbutz Lochamei Haghettaot (Ghetto Fighters Kibbutz). These are only a few of the many Jewish women who fought for the dignity of the Jewish people during World War II. Certainly it would be impossible here to document completely the role of Jewish women in Holocaust resistance. Those we mention are symbolic of those no less brave -- some of whose names and deeds we may indeed never know.

Although most fighting women were involved in mixed resistance groups, there were also some exclusively for women -- most notable was the women's group in Ravensbruck concentration camp led by Olga Benario and Charlotte Eisenbletter. Abraham Lissner, a French partisan, described two such groups:

> Since September, 1942 there has been in Paris a group of Jewish women partisans, part of the Jewish Partisan Unit.... They carry out sabotage acts, using time bombs and grenades.

A later entry in his diary describes a special team of women who study the movement of German military groups by wandering the streets of Paris.

The task of courier was one of the most vital and dangerous jobs in the resistance since the courier was the only contact with the outside world. The courier led people out of the ghetto, smuggled in food and medicine, guns and explosives. Women were ideal for this role. If she had the proper documents, accent, and Aryan features, she needed only keep calm upon questioning. A Jewish man, on the other hand, could easily be found out because of his circumcision.

Two Famous Couriers

Two famous couriers were Liza Magum of Vilna and Sima of the Minsk Ghetto. Liza, caught at 23 by a Lithuanian policeman and handed over to the Gestapo, was tortured to death, but did not betray her comrades. Her name was later used as a signal for partisan mobilization "Liza Ruft" ("Lisa Calls"). Sima, only 12, led many Jews to the forest from the Minsk ghetto. Of her it was said, "no assignment was too difficult."

In the Soviet Union, there were at least some women members in almost every partisan detachment although they usually numbered no more than 2 or 3%, and rarely more than 5%. In nearly every resistance band where Jews were active, Jewish women were involved. Chiefly they were used as scouts and intelligence agents. Soviet intelligence tended to rely heavily on women agents, particularly in partisan-infested territory where women made the best agents since men of military age were liable to arrest on sight.

In Russia most Gentile partisan women were volunteers motivated by either political conviction (some were staunch Communists) or a desire for adventure or the wish to achieve some form of personal fulfillment in a society where satisfying personal success outside the role of mother and wife was greatly limited.

The Soviet Union actively recruited women in various aspects of its armed forces, and heavily publicized participation of its women in partisan activities as evidence of superior dedication and resolution. With the loss of so many men (Russia eventually lost over 13 million soldiers), its women were crucial in the anti-fascist war effort.

One Jewish woman, for example, was awarded the title "Hero of the Soviet Union," according to Eckman and Lazar in their book, The Jewish Resistance. Zenia

Eichenbaum, who joined the Slonim Group 51 Partisans at age 14, starting as a nurse, went on to participate in all major partisan operations of the Schors Detachment. A fearless railway miner, in August 1943 at only 18, she was on the way to blow up the Brest-Pinsk railway track when they encountered an enemy ambush. When the group started to retreat she yelled, "Cowards, where are you running! Forward! Forward!" The partisans then rushed the Germans, who then fled. On March 32, 1944, before the arrival of the Red army, this "courageous girl" was killed in battle against retreating Germans.

Some of the partisan women had training as radio operators and nurses and a large proportion of the doctors assigned to the partisan units were also women. Sometimes the women were assigned to combat missions along with the men but it appears that aside from intelligence missions, they were more likely to be used as medical personnel, cooks, and washerwomen. This was as true for Jewish groups as for non-Jewish.

On the other hand the Germans saw enlistment of women for combat duty as an outright abomination. In German eyes, women were for "Kirche, Kueche, and Kinder" ("Church, Kitchen, and Children"). Yet even such "sexist pigs" as the Germans were forced to enlist women intelligence gatherers in certain occupied territories toward the end of the war.

Some of the Problems

My father, Irving Porter, was an assistant commander in the Kruk Division of partisans fighting in the area of Volynhia in the Western Ukraine, and my mother, Faye Merin Porter, was the chief cook for the detachment. They have told me some of the problems plaguing women partisans.

Sexism abounded. Even those women who did go out on missions to engage the enemy, to blow up bridges, lay mines along the railway tracks, or to simply gather food and clothing from local peasants, were often asked to wash the dishes or mend socks after returning to base camp! Then, as now, women served "double-duty." They were first seen as women, not as soldiers.

During war-time, men often act like beasts. Rape and degradation are common. A woman needed a man to protect her. Quite often, women married during and after the war, not out of love, but out of convenience - simply in order to survive or to be able to emigrate out of Europe. To be sure, these were not "matches made in heaven" and the incompatibility of the partners was quite evident. For the sake of the children or because of social and religious pressure, these couples stayed together while sleeping in separate beds for many years. In some cases, their own children were not even aware of this set of circumstances.

Earl Ziemke, in his chapter on the "Composition and Morale of the Partisan Movement" in Soviet Partisans in World War II (John A. Armstrong, ed.) notes with some cynicism that among non-Jews the principle reason for including women in nearly every detachment was that a woman became one of the prerequisites (read: possessions) of every major partisan officer, along with his Nagan pistol and leather windbreaker. It was not unusual for the officers, from brigade commander to battalion commander to "marry" the women enlisted in their unit. Jealousy was common, and fights, some leading to death, often broke out over the possession of a woman. These women became the "property" of the commanders which by implication gave them officer status, and thus the commander's "wife" often lorded it over the other women and lower-ranking men.

Whether or not the Jewish heroines of the partisan ghettos and death camp resistance were treated in a sexist fashion is generally not discussed; the stories that have come down to us are of valor and martyrdom.

In Italy, for example, according to Yuri Suhl, "The Jewish women in the partisan movement distinguished themselves for their self-sacrifice and dedication. The only woman to fall in battle, 23-year-old Rita Rosani, participated in the bitterest battles. She died fighting September 14, 1944." Posthumously awarded the golden medal for bravery, a monument was erected in the place she fell; in Verona a street was named after her and a monument stands in her honor in the memorial park in Trieste.

The "Most Famous"

But the most famous of the partisan women was Hannah Senesh, a young Jewish poet and parachutist for the Haganah. One of her fellow parachutists, Reuven Dafne, depicted her as a "spiritual girl guided almost

by mysticism. Perhaps one can say she had charisma ...
she was fearless, dauntless, stubborn." She was "a
heroine." Dropped behind enemy lines to gather
intelligence, set up radio communications, and organize
internal resistance, she was captured and executed by
the Nazis on November 7, 1944, along with several other
Jewish fighters, including Havivah Reich, another woman
in the Haganah. Altogether, 32 Palestinian parachutists were dropped behind enemy lines, three of them
women.

Tzivia Lubetkin, the most famous of the "mothers"
in the ghettos, played a key role in the Warsaw Ghetto
Uprising. An organizer of the Jewish Fighting Organization and member of the High Command along with Mordecai Anielewicz, Samuel Breslau, Mordecai Tenenbaum and
her husband, Yitzhak (Antek) Zuckerman, she played such
a central role that her name was used as the code word
for the life of the Jews in Poland in the entire underground correspondence of the period. Since statements
such as "Mendl had gone to see Tzivia" or "Tzivia is
very sick" had to be self-explanatory to the recipients
of letters, this use of her name was an unusual, spon-
taneous kind of tribute to the nature and extent of her
involvement. When the ghetto was liquidated, she
escaped through the sewers to the forest and joined the
partisans. In 1960 she was a key witness in the Eich-
mann Trial. At her death, the Warsaw Ghetto Resistance
Organization paid tribute to "this member of the heroic
leadership of the Ghetto Uprising, a pillar of strength
in those dark and hopeless days during the Holocaust."

Infiltration and assassination were frequently
done by Jewish women since Germans were taken off guard
by young girls who looked Aryan. Meta, a Dutch Jewess,
worked as a typist for the Gestapo in Paris. According
to Marie Syrkin (Blessed is the Match), this type of
work was extremely dangerous.

Halina Mazanik of the Minsk underground assassinated the infamous General Kube, while she worked in
his house as a domestic, by placing a time bomb, she
had received from another woman partisan, under his
bed. She escaped with her family to the partisans in
the forest.

"Wanda With the Braids"

"Wanda," the underground name of Niuta Teitelboim, was notorious as an assassin and saboteur. A slim, attractive blonde of 24, Wanda looked 16 when she wore her hair in braids. Her method was to walk into the office of a high-ranking German officer, shoot him in cold blood, and walk out nonchalantly. For this reason, she was on the most-wanted list of the Gestapo, who called her "Die Kleine Wanda mit die Zopfen" (little Wanda with the braids). Wanda also organized a women's unit in the Warsaw Ghetto and was a weapons instructor to one cell. She later left the ghetto to become deputy commander of the Partisan Special Task Force of Warsaw and volunteered for the most dangerous sabotoge missions. When finally captured in 1943, she tried to poison herself in lieu of undergoing the Gestapo torture chambers but, failing in the attempt, smuggled a message to her comrades reassuring them of her unflagging loyalty to them.

Rosa (Shoshana) Robota, a heroine of the Auschwitz underground and a member of the Sonderkommando (Jews who were camp workers), was among several women who were responsible for blowing up one of the four crematoria in Birkenau, the women's sector of Auschwitz. Rosa's particular task was to smuggle dynamite -- which she did in small match boxes -- for the construction of bombs. The resistors tossed a sadistic German overseer in the oven before blowing it up, killed four SS men, and wounded a number of others. They then cut the barbed wire fence and about 600 inmates escaped. Most of them were hunted down by the SS and shot. This action was the only armed revolt in the history of Auschwitz. Rosa was caught and died at the age of 21, in October 1944, by hanging, along with several other women. Before her death after days of torture, she wrote a message on her cell wall: Hazak v'amatx, Hebrew for "Be strong and brave," and that she was. A fellow member of the underground who visited Rosa's cell before her hanging learned that she had shouldered all the blame and had implicated none of her co-conspirators.

One of Rosa's cohorts in the crematorium bombing project who was also captured at the same time was Rachel Baum. An extraordinarily beautiful girl, Rachel was raped in 1942 at the age of 18 by a Nazi party boss in central Poland, and witnessed her father's murder when he tried to attack the rapist. She and the other surviving members of her family were then shipped to Birkenau, where she joined the underground. After their revolt and arrest, Rachel survived four days of brutal whipping and torture and had her hands and feet crushed. When she was carried to the gallows, she used her last ounce of strength to stand on her mangled feet and call to the amassed prisoners, "My people -- avenge me!"

Another heroine of Auschwitz was Mala Zimetbaum. Born in Poland in 1920, she later lived in Belgium and was a member of another Zionist movement, Hanoar Hatzioni. At Auschwitz, she was a "runner," interpreter, and member of the underground resistance. She too was captured, tortured, but died a heroine's death, without revealing the names of others, on August 22, 1944.

In conclusion, one cannot minimize the heroic role of Jewish women during the war. This article can only hint at the heroism demonstrated. As one partisan wrote: "They were not extraordinary women. They were not exceptions. (They) had a daily heroism."

                                                    1978

A Selected Bibliography

Ainsztein, Reuben, _Jewish Resistance in Nazi-Occupied Eastern Europe_, Barns and Noble, N.Y. (Harper and Row), A monumental study of Jewish resistance.

Lester Eckman and Chaim Lazar, _The Jewish Resistance._ Shengold Publishers, 1977. $10.00/282 pp. The history of the Jewish partisans in Lithuania and White Russia during the Nazi occupation.

Syrkin, Marie, _Blessed in the Match: The Story of Jewish Resistance_, Philadelphia: Jewish Publication Society, 1948. One of the first accounts of Hannah Senesh and other examples of Jewish resistance. It should be read in conjunc tion with her own memoirs, _Her Life and Diary_, Schocken, N.Y. 1973.

Sisters in Exile: Sources on the Jewish Woman, New York: Ichud Habonim Labor Zionist Youth (575 Sixth Ave., NYC), no date. A collection of source material on Jewish women from a socialist-Zionist point of view, available in paperback from the above address. Contains a selection from the memoirs of Tzivia Lubetkin, dealing with the last days of the Warsaw Ghetto.

Suhl, Yuri (tr. and ed.), _The Story of the Jewish Resistance in Nazi Europe_, N.Y.: Schocken, paper back, 1975. Originally published by Crown Pub lishers in hardcover this paperback is more recent. Contains material on Rosa Robota (pages 210-225) and Mala Zimetbaum, another heroine of the Auschwitz underground (pages 182-188).

Ziemke, Earl, "Compositon and Morale of the Partisan Movement" in John A. Armstrong (ed.), _Soviet Partisans in World War II_, University of Wisconsin Press, Madison, Wis. 1964, $27.50, hardcover. Intended for scholars in the field; highly reli able analyses based on captured German documents. The author has relied heavily on the work of Ziemke on the role of women in the partisan move ment (pages 147-148).

ON THERAPY, RESEARCH AND OTHER DANGEROUS PHENOMENA

With the recent upsurge of interest in the Holocaust because of the NBC-TV special, there has also been an increase in the number of Holocaust survivor's groups, therapy groups, discussion groups, and research on such groups especially as it relates to the children of survivors. Psychologists have found a rare species of animal that they have overlooked -- the children of survivors -- and they are going after them vigorously. They will question them, tag them, give them all kinds of erudite clinical labels, and publish the results in the most prestigious psychiatric journals. Beware! They might not have the slightest idea of where they tread. (How could they? It's such a new field!) Worse they may even cause psychological damage and suffering if they are callous, ill-trained, or unprofessional.

I would like to discuss two of these areas -- psychological research on the children of survivors and so-called therapy groups for these same children. (Children is a misnomer; nearly all of these "children" are by now over 18, and most are in their mid-20's to late 30's).

* * * *

Most of the research on survivors and their children is from a psychological point of view, and little of it is done from the much broader perspective of sociology, politics, or religion. This is not to deny that there is much research on the psychological problems of survivors and their children that is valuable, but it is only valuable on a case-by-case approach. Psychiatrists have agreed that there is a survivor's syndrome, a collection of problems (anxiety, nightmares, depression, psycho-somatic ailments, etc.) that survivors tend to have. I would be very surprised if they didn't have them after what they had gone through. I agree that such a syndrome exists, but now psychiatrists are beginning to talk of a syndrome among the children of survivors, of terrible afflictions and maladies that are to befall them. They can tentatively call it a syndrome, but they have not the slightest bit of evidence to prove it. There are two powerful biases in much of the psychiatric literature on survivors and their children:

It is automatically biased toward pathology, which always seems to stress the negative

-79-

aspects of any "syndrome". What about the
positive side of being a Holocaust victim?
What about the strengths, both psychological
and otherwise, that survivors and their
children have? And finally, what about most
of the survivors who are psychologically
stable, even healthy? One never sees this
perspective in the literature.

It is biased methodologically. All of the
studies I have read have extremely small
samples -- six patients here, 17 survivors
there, 22 somewhere else. Any statistician
can tell you that one cannot generalize about
all survivors or their children from such
small samples. The only way to make generalizations is to have a sample of at least 100
survivors, 100 children of survivors, and an
equal number of a control group, such as
American-born Jews. Such research, if it
contained psychological tests as well as
sociological questionnaires, would easily
cost $20,000 or more. Until such a large
sample is undertaken, there can be few
generalizations about survivors that will
have any validity.

But we do need research. We need psychological
case studies. They are useful, but we need more
sociology, political science, and anthropology graduate
students and their teachers engaged in studies such as
the sociology of "New American" clubs, the differences
between the ways that Israel deals with survivors and
the Holocaust when compared to Diaspora countries, the
meaning that the Holocaust has for Jewish children, and
a host of other studies. I believe we have had enough
psychiatric studies, and I am tired of being a guinea
pig for yet another psycho-analyst.

* * * *

In line with the rise of children of survivor's
groups, such as One Generation After in Boston and The
Generation After in New York, has come therapy groups
for the children. I have been in such therapy groups,
and my experience has been mixed. First, on the positive side, the people who led them were sincere and
dedicated. I would not wish to deprecate them and
their efforts. (They are usually children of survivors
themselves.) Everyone in the field is well-intentioned

-- but they can still do harm! Secondly, there is nothing wrong with discussion groups, "rap" groups, and similar get-togethers of children of survivors. These can be both educational and healthy. To meet people who have had similar experiences or similar parents or similar interests can be refreshing.

Some of these so-called therapy groups can never decide exactly what they are. First of all, some of the therapists are ill-trained and professionally imma- ture. The Holocaust is a complex trauma and needs a highly experienced and mature therapist. Secondly, these ad-hoc groups contain people who do not need therapy or have already had intensive therapy. People of diverse psychological backgrounds and needs are thrown together and the result can be confusing at best and harmful at worst. Third, many therapists have not carefully formulated the goals for such groups. If sensitive matter is raised and someone in the group is deeply agitated by it, there is little follow-up or referral to another therapist or to the same therapist. Finally, some people are let into such "therapy" groups only to discover that they are being used as research subjects for someone's practicum or master's thesis.

I could go on with other abuses but enough said. As in nearly every other aspect of this society, the survivor-consumer must heed the advice of <u>caveat</u> <u>emp- tor</u>. It is good that the helping professions have been made aware of survivors and their children, but like the sensitivity-encounter movement of the late 60's, these new survivor therapies also have their share of incompetents.

The response to this editorial was immediate but surprisingly not on the subject of therapy groups and their lack of professionalism. Most people seemed to agree with me. Where I did receive heavy criticism was from scholars in the field (such as Professor Leo Eitinger of Oslo and Haifa) who questioned that the sample size of survivors and their children were small and inadequate in number. Professor Eitinger gave examples (in <u>Shoah</u>, Vol. 2, No. 1, Spring-Summer, 1980 issue) of research that contained samples of 1,000, 6,000, and nearly 20,000. I stand corrected on the survivors but I will continue to maintain that the samples of the children of survivors are still small. We definitely need a large, comparative, cross-sectional sample of them. Another point that Professor Eitinger made which is salient is that the early post-World War II studies stressed the pathological in order to counteract the prevailing view that the Jewish trauma was minimal, that mental illness was endogenous and innate, and that restitution was not necessary for the victims. It was through the fine work of Professor Eitinger and his colleagues that so may Jews and non-Jews were able to receive <u>Widergutmachen</u>. I learned a great deal from the response to the article, and a more balanced view of psychiatry emerged on my part. In fact, ironically, I belong to a study group on the children of survivors at the Boston Psychoanalytic Society!

1979

IS THERE A SURVIVOR'S SYNDROME?
PSYCHOLOGICAL AND SOCIO-POLITICAL IMPLICATIONS

An analysis of the children of survivors and their parents through the use of sociological observation and examination of the literature is presented, showing that there exists a psychological survivor's syndrome among the victims of the Holocaust. Also, the basis for a socio-political syndrome is indicated. As for the children of survivors, most of whom are now between 20-35 years of age, there is not enough data to say for sure, but it is highly unlikely that a pathological syndrome exists, though a mild secondary guilt syndrome may appear in some cases. More research with larger samples is necessary. As for a socio-political syndrome, superficial observation yields that a large number of children of survivors are committed to making sense out of the Holocaust and this can lead to a wide variety of creative political and religious actions. Also presented are some observations on the third generation of survivors, the offspring of the children of the original survivors.

* * * *

The purpose of this paper is to present a survey of the highlights of the socio-psychological literature concerning the aftereffects of the Holocaust upon survivors and their children, and to answer the question whether there exists a "survivor's syndrome" among both survivors and their children. Furthermore, this paper will introduce a new concept, the socio-political syndrome among survivors and their offspring. In short, it will try to answer the question whether one can generalize about a socio-political syndrome as well as a psychological syndrome among these two groups.

Literature in this area divides into two parts, each overlapping the other; psycho-analytical case studies written by psychologists and psychiatrists and personal memoirs or journalistic accounts written by survivors themselves or by sympathetic writers. Though a significant body of literature exists, most of it is based on small clinical samples. There is a great deal of work to be done not only by psychologists but by sociologists and political scientists in order to expand our knowledge of survivors. Researchers in the past too often emphasized severe pathology not only of the first generation but the second generation of survivors as well. This paper questions whether a "pathological" approach is sufficient. It proposes that social psychological and sociological studies be developed in order to examine those survivors and their children who function normally and who are not beset by severe psychological problems. In other words, the socio-political aspects of these groups must also be examined in order to round out the picture of the Holocaust survivors.

Disaster Studies: An Overview

Generally, studies of the Holocaust victims fall under the broad category of disaster research. These studies contain several labels -- "trauma research," "stress or seige studies," "collective behavior," "catastrophe studies," and "disaster research." There are four major approaches which scientists take (Grossen, Welchsler, and Greenblatt, 1969).

General Systems Theory is concerned with the structure and process of systems of social phenomena. The concepts of adaptation to stress, equilibrium maintenance in reaction to such stress, information-processing, inputs, and outputs are all used in this approach. General systems theory is useful in precisely defining and manipulating social variables within a given system, especially through the use of computers and statistical models. It is an important tool in research and should be used more widely in this field but I find the approach too mechanical and consequently will not use it in this discussion.

Collective Behavior Theory is another popular approach to disaster studies. Collective behavior is actually a generic term for various social phenomena; crowds, riots, revolts, propaganda, public opinion, mass migration, and natural and man-made disasters. Such an approach emphasizes group morale, leadership, cohesiveness, collective defense, rumor control, and other manifestations of group behavior. This theoretical approach is also a useful tool but will not be stressed in this article.

Socio-Political Theory emphasizes the sociological, religious, cultural, political, and economic adaptations of survivors and victims to disaster. This approach will be widely used in the discussion of a possible "socio-political syndrome" among survivors and their children. This approach places the survivor in his/her normal socio-economic setting after the Holocaust and stresses the positive rather than the pathological adaptations of the victims.

Psycho-analytical Theory puts its major emphasis on individual reactions to stressful situations. The vocabulary of this approach concentrates on such concepts as trauma, emotional reaction, threat, defense, anxiety, guilt, and internal conflict. It is both a therapeutic and analytical approach; that is, it is both therapy and theory. Bruno Bettelheim, Viktor Frankl, Elie Cohen, Robert J. Lifton, William Niederland, Judith Kestenberg, H.Z. Winnik, Vivian Rakoff and John Sigal are the most widely-read figures in this field. This approach will be used in this paper in describing the "psychological syndrome" of survivors and their children.

One danger is to rely solely upon one approach. Each perspective gives only one view of the subject. It is necessary to utilize as many approaches as possible in order to obtain a complete picture. For example, the weakness of much of the Holocaust research is that it is rarely comparative. Concentration camp research is actually a subcategory of research on such total institutions as military prisons, POW camps, and civilian prisons. If Jews in such camps were compared to soldiers in POW camps, a more balanced and less defensive perspective could emerge. If the Jewish reaction to ghettoization and persecution were compared to reactions of civilians to such diverse phenomena as nuclear attack, natural disasters, air-raids, and collective panic, then research would show that the Jews reacted similarly to other groups (Grosser, Welchsler, and Greenblatt, 1964). If Jewish survivors could be compared to Armenian or Gypsy survivors, again a more balanced picture could be drawn. In short, the appearance of guilt and other psychological reactions are as normal for survivors of the Holocaust as they are for survivors of nuclear attack, natural disasters, war combat, or intense life-depriving accidents such as plane or car crashes.

What is a Survivor?

Before the outbreak of World War II, there were about 8.8 million Jews living in Europe. Approximately 5.8-6.2 million Jews were killed in the Holocaust. Of

the three million who remained, it has been estimated
that between 400,000-500,000 survived the war years in
labor camps, in the partisans, hiding in caves, in the
forests or the countryside. No more than 75,000 outlived the concentration camps (Epstein, 1977). Thus,
there are about a half million or three million survivors depending on one's definition. I will adhere to
the half-million figure: that is, a survivor is someone who has survived an immediate and traumatic life-
threatening experience. Otherwise, one could say that
all Jews everywhere were survivors because it was the
Nazi aim to exterminate all of them. But this, while
true in a metaphorical sense, would only confuse the
issue.

We could say that there are about one-half million
children of survivors in the world, the majority of
them between 25-35 years old. Their parents range in
age from 55 to 75, assuming they were between 20-40
years old when the war ended in 1945. The largest
number of survivors went to live in Israel, with many
coming to the United States and Canada, and with other
large pockets of survivors in South America, England,
France, and the Soviet Union. Many of these survivors
and their children live in distinct communities set
apart not only from the non-Jewish, but also from the
already established Jewish community.

The label of survivor will be used for anyone who
experienced life-threatening traumas and who left
Europe in the 1930's -- mostly German and Austrian
Jews, as well as those who went through the DP camp
experience and left in the late 1940's and early 1950's
for Israel, Canada, the Americas, or other countries.
The children of survivors are defined as those who are
the offspring of survivors, whether or not these
children experienced the Nazi trauma first-hand or not.
That is, it includes those born in Europe during the
war, those born in DP camps after the war, and those
born in the "new" country long after the war.

This paper will outline the psychological symptoms
of survivors and the socio-political coping behaviors
of first-generation survivors. It will then explore
the psychological and then the socio-political coping
behavior of the children of survivors. Some feel that
the Nazi trauma is re-experienced in the lives of the
children and even the grandchildren of survivors. Is
this true only for those who were death camp survivors
or for all types of survivors? What is the magnitude,

severity, and duration of these effects? How are these effects passed on to future generations? It may not be possible to answer all these questions in this paper, but they will be raised so that others can find an answer.

Clinical Symptomology of Holocaust Survivors

Psychiatrists have attempted to explain whether or not there exists an entity called the "survivor syndrome" and if so, what are its manifestations. One of the world's foremost authorities on psychic trauma, William G. Niederland, has outlined some of the primary and secondary characteristics of adults on whom repeated traumata has been inflicted (in Krystal & Niederland, 1971).

> Personality changes in the survivor of such experiences are related to quantitative factors. Massive traumatic experiences of this kind have devastating effects on the total ego organization. Most survivors suffer from chronic or recurrent depressive reactions often accompanied by states of anxiety, phobic fears, nightmares, somatic equivalents, and brooding ruminations about the past and lost-love objects.

> The sequelae of massive and repeated traumatization are:

> 1. Anxiety, usually associated with phobic or hypochondriacal fears, alone or in combination.

> 2. Disturbances of cognition and memory.

> 3. Chronic depressive reactions characterized by guilt, seclusion, and isolation.

> 4. Psychosomatic symptoms or disorders.

> 5. Psychosis-like psychotic manifestations.

> 6. Life-long sense of heightened vulnerability to and increased awareness of dangerous situations.

> 7. Disturbances of sense identity, body-image, and self-image.

8. Permanent personality changes. (pp. 1-9)

Let us examine in more detail what Niederland calls the sequelae or aftereffects of traumatization.

Anxiety. This is the most common complaint and is associated with fear of renewed persecution. Victims manifest deep disturbances, phobias, anxiety dreams, and rerun nightmares. Chronic insomnia occurs due to these recurrent nightmares and anxieties.

Disturbances of cognition and memory. Amnesia, especially upon waking up from nightmares, is the most prevalent disturbance here. Lost or bewildered states and a sense of disorientation from the present are also found.

Chronic depressive reactions. These reactions, from masochistic character changes to psychotic depression, cover a wide range. In their severity, the reactions are correlated to the intensity of survivor guilt based on the loss of loved ones.

Tendency to isolation, withdrawal, and brooding. Survivors are marked by unstable or difficult relationships and problems with intimacy. These psychological states manifest themselves in other social set--tings and victims often withdraw from political and community involvement.

Alterations of personal identity. These include impairment of body image and self-image and manifest themselves in frequent complaints of "I am a different person," "I am a weaker, more abhorrent person," or in some cases, "I am not a person." At its most extreme, the image of the musselman or living corpse appearance which some victims exhibit is an example of this alteration. Robert Lifton makes similar statements about Hiroshima survivors who exhibit a kind of psychic numbing, a closing-off of feelings, manifested by a macabre, shadowy, shuffling, and ghost-like impression. The all-encompassing psychological scar on the total personality is often a defense against death anxiety and death guilt. In milder forms it appears as sluggish despair consisting of diminished vitality, easy fatigability, "weakness," exhaustion" of the nervous system, and "inadequate functioning of an organ system of the body." One must however be careful with facile comparisons between a sudden event like nuclear attack as in Hiroshima and long-term trauma as in concentration camp life.

Psychosomatic conditions. Such conditions are quite common and form the basis for many German restitution claims. They can exhibit themselves immediately after liberation for the trauma or many years later. Research is needed to find out if there is a "ticking-clock" syndrome -- illnesses induced by the Nazi experience 20, 30, or 40 years after the event. These conditions include diseases related to chronic states of tension or anger; gastrointestinal conditions, peptic ulcers, and related symptoms; cardiovascular disturbances such as angina pectoris, heart disease, etc.; cancer; and the typical survivor triad of headaches, persistent nightmares, and chronic depression accompanied by various psychosomatic complaints.

Psychotic and psychotic-like states. These occur in the most extreme cases of survivor traumata. Regressive and primitive methods of dealing with aggression can result in schizophrenic-like symptoms such as hallucinations, fantasy-building, states of depersonalization, hypochondriatic symptoms, or paranoid manifestations, all having a very specific history and determination.

Conclusion. Research in the field definitely shows that Holocaust survivors do manifest a psychological survivor syndrome with at minimum, the survivor triad mentioned above, and at maximum, the more pathological problems stated above. It should be emphasized however that most survivors have adapted quite well to their traumatic experience and live fairly normal lives. Psychologists tend to generalize from small clinical samples and emphasize only the pathological. They should take a cue from Abraham Maslow and begin to balance the picture with case studies of the strengths and self-affirmations of Holocaust survivors. They too often dwell only on the negative. Research on the positive aspects of "survivorship" should be encouraged.

Coping Behavior of Survivors: Social and Political Adaptations

The study now moves away from psychological studies into the realm of sociology. Research on the sociology of Holocaust survivors and their children is almost non-existent. While there is some literature on the socio-political acculturation of immigrant groups to

America, the following section is a first step towards a description of socio-political adaptation of specifically post-World War II Holocaust survivors. What follows is a brief series of observations and hypotheses that require more quantitative verification. The observations are generalized from the survivor community of Milwaukee, Wisconsin, where I lived from 1948-1968, and I discuss an Ashkenazic, Eastern European milieu. Other survivor communities, such as those composed of Sephardic or Austro-German Holocaust survivors, would differ in some respects from this sample in the areas of education, religiosity, assimilation, and other factors.

Jewish survivors of the Holocaust are also new immigrants to their host country, whether that be Israel, the USA, Canada, England, or Argentina. The burden of adapting to a new life style, language, and culture is added to the already heavy burden of the Holocaust trauma. The kind of adjustment they make to their new homeland depends on many variables. Among these are family situation, maturity, age, level of education, job opportunities, religious background, support of relatives and social agencies, and support from within the community of survivors.

Despite all the difficulties, most survivors have adjusted quite well. Financially, they are fairly secure; some have even become quite wealthy in the short time they have been in America. Doing fairly well does not mean that in terms of occupational status and prestige, survivors have moved far up the social ladder, but they have done better than expected given generally low levels of education and training. Many of the Russian and Polish Jews of Milwaukee went into marginal trades; tailors, caterers, scrap metal, or used auto parts dealers, mom and pop grocery stores, and garment industry jobs. A few became Hebrew teachers, cantors, sextons, and rabbis. Engineers, doctors, dentists, and professors are virtually non-existent in this community. German and Austrian Jews, on the other hand, because of their education and training were more likely to be engaged in law, medicine, or other professions.

Like most American immigrants, survivors desired for their children the utmost in schooling, and for the most part they succeeded. Within a single generation, their children very nearly caught up occupationally and educationally with their host-country contemporaries.

A great many survivor-children married non-survivor children and with their advanced training and education, they entered into professions such as teaching, social work, law, accounting, or business. A few joined their parents in the family business, a fact that their parents viewed as a step-down in prestige even though these same children are much better off financially than if they had gone into, for example, teaching.

Most parents expected their children to surpass them in education and occupational mobility, and though this caused some tension between generations, it was an accepted fact. Many survivor-parents sacrificed their lives for the sake of their children's careers. This kind of sacrifice is not new in American Jewish history. It occurred at the turn of the century during the great waves of immigration from Europe, and Jewish parents have been sacrificing ever since. It will be interesting to see whether the second generation of children will sacrifice for their children.

Survivor-parents of the Milwaukee Jewish community number about 1,000 out of a total of 24,000 Jews, and they tend to cluster around six synagogues, four of them Orthodox, on the northwest side of the city. Their children and even a growing number of the parents have moved to the east or northeast part of town, a more affluent section, yet they retain their ties to the "old" Jewish neighborhood. While some parents may be non-observant, or even anti-observant, most continue to live in the religious community and observe traditions out of respect for the memory of their parents or because they truly believe in their Orthodox life style. They know no other. The relationship to their rabbis -- two of the <u>shuls</u> are led by Hasidic <u>rebbes</u>, is the same one they maintained in their <u>shetlach</u> and cities in Eastern Europe. As one rabbi told me: "I didn't leave Rovno; I brought it with me here and built an American Rovno in Milwaukee."

Politically, survivors tend to be somewhat passive and conservative. They keep a low profile, rarely becoming involved in city, state or national politics. They try to avoid controversy, political or otherwise. Given their previous experiences, this conservatism is understandable. But another reason may simply be that they see themselves, even after thirty years in the country, as greenhorns. They are often ashamed of how they speak English, or how they act or dress. They feel that they are too ignorant of the political process to become involved, or that they will look foolish. Some are deeply suspicious and even mortally afraid of authority figures, whether policemen, politicians, or petty bureaucrats. Their children do not suffer from this fear.

Some survivors try to assimilate into the general Jewish community, and a tiny few into the general Christian population, but the vast majority seem most comfortable with their own kind. They feel that not only non-Jews but even other Jews do not really understand them or their past traumas. They react to their Americanized children in the same way. At times, neither the survivor nor the kin understands the other. Sometimes, the kin are ashamed of the survivor, and even feel the survivor is guilty for having survived.

In two areas, however, survivors are politically involved and their involvement comes with such force and devotion, that it sometimes shocks non-survivor Jews. These areas are the fate of Israel and the plight of Soviet Jewry. Survivors are very active in various fund-raising activities for these two causes, either within their synagogues or through survivor organizations such as the New American Club. These clubs should be studied more intensively. They form the nucleus of social activity for many survivors with their dances, raffles, and fund-raising events. These clubs are an opportunity for survivors to relax, speak Yiddish, and enjoy oneself in the company of a close-knit community of survivors. In fact, it is only at these clubs and at family events (weddings, bar mitzvot, a bris-circumcision) that I have seen survivors relax and temporarily forget their past traumas.

Their ties with Israel are extremely close, not only spiritually, but socially. Many survivors have relatives in Israel and there is much contact between them. Israel is crucial to survivors psychologically as one of the few havens for Jews anywhere in the world. A disproportionate number of them support militant pro-Israeli groups such as the Jewish Defense League or the Revisionist Zionists, though many are ambivalent about the violence associated with these two groups. Many survivors also join and support the Pioneer Women, Farband, and other Labor Zionist groups and, if Orthodox, they will support the Mizrachi (Religious) Zionist organizations.

Survivors, like other Jews, have been staunch Democratic Party supporters from the time of President Truman. While there was some slippage toward the Republicans and to Richard Nixon in 1972, this was because Senator George McGovern, Nixon's opponent, was thought to have been soft in his support of Israel. In the future, too, it seems that survivors will support those candidates that are firm in their defense of Israel regardless of the candidate's other positions.

Conclusions

There is much more that one could say about the sociology and politics of survivors. We can conclude that these survivors tend to live in tightly-knit survivor communities which consist of others who speak the same language, carry on the same customs of the Old Country, of the shtetl or the urban ghetto of Europe. They live a richly traditional but quiet life apart from other Jews in the community, and they donate much of their limited energies to their shul, their rabbi, Israeli causes, and the lives of their children and grandchildren. They work very hard, sometimes too hard, perhaps in order to try and forget the past. They are politically active and quite concerned, even paranoid, about anti-Semitism and about Israel.

There is a socio-political "syndrome" that one can generalize. Survivors do share many common sociological features. Quotes around the word "syndrome" are used because the common dictionary meaning of the word is that of a complex or a group of traits that are abnormal and/or undesirable. The meaning of the term "syndrome" has been changed to include in this case a group of traits that are positive and normal; in other words, syndrome is used to mean any group of shared traits or features. In this sense, survivors do share a socio-political syndrome as well as a psychological one, and future studies must be social-psychological in the sense they begin to understand the survivor and the children within the context of, and not in isolation from, the community.

Coping Behavior of Survivor-Children: Psychological Adaptations

Who precisely is a child of survivors? Judith Kestenberg, an American psychiatrist who has done extensive research in this area, defines the child of survivors as "one who was born after the Holocaust or has not been himself subjected to persecution or maltreatment" (1972, p. 323). Though this definition is fine for now, a more complex one may be needed to also convey the impact of escape, migration, and childhood development in a family of survivors as well as the direct persecution by the Nazis. The subsequent post-war experience in DP camps can also lead to psychological conflicts. Kestenberg's definition is adequate even though it spreads over a large net of survivor-children, yet it technically leaves out those who have been subjected to persecution or maltreatment. I suppose these children could then be considered both survivors and children of survivors. In any case, Kestenberg's definition will prove adequate for this discussion.

In the past few years, there has been an increased interest in the children of survivors by psychologists and by the children themselves. One should really call them young adults rather than children because most of them are now between 20 and 35 years old and are at an age where they are forming groups of survivors' children in order to discuss the implications of their self-identity. A few years ago there was not a great deal of data on the subject except for several symposia and scattered articles, all of them emphasizing the psychoanalytical impact. However, the children of survivors themselves have begun to write about their experiences and have initiated research on the topic. Much of the earlier psychiatric literature is sketchy and has small clinical samples. Also, the non-psychiatric writings are impressionistic. However, new research should soon reveal if a psychological syndrome exists among the offspring of survivors and what its parameters are. It seems, however, that with some pathological exceptions, there appears to be a mild syndrome in the making; nothing that should alarm people, but enough of a syndrome to study and evaluate.

Kestenberg herself believed (in 1972) that there was no specific syndrome among children of survivors but she was cautious about closing the book on the subject. A rather bizarre and exceptional case had forced her to keep the question open:

> Some years ago I analyzed a young adolescent
> who behaved in a bizarre way, starving him-
> self, hiding in woods and treating me ... as

a hostile persecutor. Soon after I connected his psychotic-like behavior with the real experiences of his parents' relatives in Europe, his symptoms abated but his analysis had to be prematurely terminated, chiefly because of his parental resistance. Haunted by the image of this patient, who came to me emaciated and hollow-eyed like a Musselman in a concentration camp, I looked at children of survivors in Israel and thought I could recognize in some faces a far away look, reminiscent of the stare of survivors of persecution. (1972, pp. 311-312)

A conclusion reached by Kestenberg was that psychiatrists themselves resisted unearthing the frightening impact of Nazi persecution on these young people. This fear appears to have abated in the past few years as more therapists are becoming aware of the need of these children to talk about their experiences.

A large number of survivors' children have sought psychiatric treatment for general problems but few therapists discuss the Holocaust as an important aspect of the child's socialization process, even though it often is an important factor.

Therapy can be of great help not only in relieving the stress of emotional conflicts but more importantly in accelerating communication between parents and child. As one child comments:

My parents never told me anything about the war .... It was like sex. You didn't talk about it in my house.... The house was like a tomb. Sometimes we went on picnics together. But underneath something was missing. (Mostysser, 1975, pp. 4-5)

What was missing was emotional contact between the generations and a deeper, cathartic sharing of the parent's fate and its effect on them as well as upon their children. Too often parents were too ashamed or afraid to discuss the subject with their offspring. They did not wish to burden their children with their sufferings and their stories. Yet the child could sense the parents' suffering while not understanding its root in the other. At times children would blame themselves for their parents' suffering and a complex web of sadness, guilt, and helplessness would develop.

Happily, more and more parents are talking to their children today. The NBC Holocaust TV special helped and the children themselves are older and more mature, more capable of initiating discussion of this formerly taboo subject. As one son of survivors recently told me: "After the NBC special, now everyone knows what I mean when I say that my parents went through the Holocaust. Everyone can share the burden a little bit, a burden that I have carried alone for over 30 years."

Eva Fogelman, a New York psychologist and a daughter of survivors, has been quoted as saying:

> I saw that psychiatrists were beginning to extend the Survivor Syndrome to us, that severe pathology was being attributed to the second generation just as it had been to our parents.... I began to feel that this was all wrong. Sure we were effected. But not to the pointed where we're not functioning normally or where we have more psychological problems than the normal population. (Epstein, 1977, p. 14)

Ms. Fogelman and her colleague Bella Savran began to run "awareness groups" for children of survivors in the spring of 1976, similar to women's consciousness-raising groups, or better yet, like rap-groups for Vietnam veterans. I would agree with Fogelman and Savran (1979) that a pathological secondary syndrome does not appear to exist, but a milder guilt syndrome may be a possibility. Robert Lifton calls this syndrome the "death imprint." Children may feel ashamed of their parent's victimization. This shame in turn can often lead to a series of conflicts within the child, between parent and child, and between the child and the outside world.

Steven Greenblatt (1978), in a study of ten children of Nazi concentration camp survivors, half of whom were engaged in some form of psychotherapy, with the other half having no such treatment, found that the clinical group expressed a great deal more emotional turmoil, were more frequently exposed to Holocaust material than the non-clinical group, and had stronger feelings of inherited attitudes, most notably more survival guilt feelings due to unresolved grief reaction, inadequate coping mechanisms, and subsequent crises proneness. One could question both the size and the reliability/validity of the sample, but it is one of a growing number of studies that is finding some kind of secondary syndrome at work.

Often the parents are so preoccupied with the unending mourning process and the problems of starting a new life in a strange country that they are unable to relate to their children's needs or respond with the necessary flexibility. The children's demands become overwhelming and are seen by parents as draining their already limited emotional resources. The parents then attack their children for not listening and for not understanding them. Often it is difficult to tell who is the child and who is the adult in these cases. Because they are unable to cope with the continuous anxious responses of their parents to their behavior, the children may either go out of control or respond by withdrawal into fantasy at best, or into an affectless state at worse (Sigal, 1971, pp. 58-59).

What are the effects on the survivor's children, if their parents raised them with few controls and with over-permissiveness, since because they had suffered so much, they could not tolerate their children being deprived in any way? If one has lost everything in the Holocaust, a parent may take no chances in making this "special" survivor-child unhappy. It fits the typical Yiddisheh Mamma, but the survivor-parent may greatly exaggerate the usual overprotectiveness of the Jewish mother. There can appear some minor forms of sado-masochism as well, with their roots in an ambivalence toward parents. They both love and are disgusted by their parents for many reasons: (a) for not being "American" or "modern" enough, and thus being ashamed of their parents; (b) seeing their parents as weak and passive before the Nazis, and thus coming into conflict with the usual image of a strong, powerful parent; (c) blaming their parents for their suffering and misery, thus setting up a round of guilt and anger and then more guilt.

Another component of a syndrome, if a syndrome does in fact exist, is the child's behavior toward authority figures, including parents, and subsequent feelings of guilt which anger and aggression toward these figures provoke. The child who has violent urges of aggression is confronted with a paradox, and either consciously or unconsciously says: "How can I attack someone who has already suffered so much?" Parents and child then turn on each other, each escalating the other's feelings of guilt. Each blames the other for their mutual sense of deprivation and frustration. A lack of communication, a blurred sense of identity, and a potential for depression can result from the dynamics of this game of guilt (Sigal, 1971, p.59).

All of this still leaves open the question of whether there is a psychological syndrome among the children of survivors. Nevertheless, any syndrome theory will have to take into account the following variables:

Age. There is some impressionable data that the first child born after the war may suffer more intensely from secondary guilt syndrome than other siblings and that all the conflicts mentioned earlier may affect him or her more than later children. The first-born child is a special child to the parents, with much promise and responsibility. It represents the rebirth of the family and the resurrection of earlier children killed by the Nazis. While the first-born may carry extra burdens, it may also be far more ambitious, successful, and creative precisely because it has been imbued with the special hopes and needs of the parents. The child may have messianic ambitions. Children born subsequently may suffer less than the first-born, but may also achieve less.

Time of birth. An important variable may be when and where the child was born; whether in the death camps, in the forest, the ghetto, the DP (displaced person) camp after the war, or later, in the host country.

Post-Holocaust experiences. These experiences are often overlooked in analysis but can prove crucial. The shock of the European liberation, the displacement from previous homes, the escape from Communist countries, the trip to the host country, the formation of new families or of families re-uniting, and adjustment to the hardships of the new country are all crucial components in any syndrome theory. The post-Holocaust phase is rarely mentioned in the literature yet can be as traumatic to survivors and their children as was the actual war-time experience.

Time of departure. Did the survivors leave before or after the war? Many German and Austrian Jews were able to leave Germany in the mid to late 1930's. Was their trauma different from the Russian or Polish Jews who managed to survive the war?

Emotional stability of parents. All persons suffered severe personal trauma during the war. The level of emotional maturity before and during the war is important in understanding to what extent the Holocaust affected parents and their children. The intactness of the family is also important. If there was a loss of a spouse, survivors tended to remarry as soon as possible after the war. These dyadic relationships were very strong even if romance or deep love was missing; often these were marriages of convenience. All these factors can affect the children.

Reaction to new stress. Adaptation after persecution is of course the key element to understanding the impact of Holocaust experiences on the children. The need to succeed and the need to work to help forget the past can lead to a tendency for over-achievement and over-involvement whether in school, business, or politics, among the children of survivors. This will be discussed in the next section.

Participation in wars of liberation. Active participation in either the regular army, the World War II resistance movements, or the Israeli wars seems to have had a beneficial effect on both survivors and their children. The channeling of feelings of powerlessness and worthlessness against a common enemy, whether Nazis or Arabs, was beneficial for mental health. The ability to take revenge was also satisfying, though never totally, since no amount of revenge could replace the loss experienced. If a parent could not fight, then vigorous support for Israel and/or for militant Jewish groups such as the JDL would suffice vicariously. Whether the parent resisted or simply hid in a cave during the war may have an important impact on the children of survivors in the sense that a sociopolitical response could develop as a result, i.e., joining the JDL or some leftist radical group as a form of continuity in resisting anti-Semitism and racism.

Conclusions

Quite likely a minor secondary guilt syndrome among the children of survivors will be found but it is too early, given the data, to say for sure. Even so, it will be mild compared to the parents. If left to the psychiatrists, they will frighten us with predictions of a severe, pathological second-generation survivor's syndrome. I do not believe that a pathology exists, and if there is a syndrome, it will be benign. A balance of the psychiatric side of the coin with sociological analyses is necessary. Such analyses will present the positive and creative side of being a child of survivors and balance the negative. Furthermore, larger samples, at least 50-100 offspring of survivors, are needed in order to generalize about all children of survivors. Without these large samples, an incomplete picture of the situation will emerge.

Coping Behavior of Survivor Children: Social and Political Adaptations

Several writers (Robert J. Lifton, Viktor Frankl, Michael Barkun) have noticed that the Holocaust, whether of Hiroshima or of Auschwitz, has imposed a sense of confusion and unspeakable horror. While some have been psychically numbed, to use Lifton's phrase, others have attempted to remake the world. Being a survivor can lead either to silence or to chivalry. The children of survivors have discovered that they must make some sense out of the Holocaust, to give this awesome and meaningless mass death some meaning. Their responses have often been creative.

According to Helen Epstein (1977, p.14), children of survivors are quite diverse. They range in age from late teens to middle-thirties and include housewives, students, teachers, business people, artists, social workers, doctors and others. They are single, married, divorced, homosexual, and heterosexual. They include strictly Orthodox and anti-religious Jews. Their political affiliations are radical, liberal, conservative, Zionist, anti-Zionist, or apolitical. They live in the cities or in the country. Some say that their parents' experience has affected them only slightly while others say that it has determined their choice of profession, friends, and spouses.

Yet despite their diversity, Epstein maintains that there is a sense of affinity among children of survivors, or as one put it: "There is a tacit understanding between us;" "A completeness without conversation," as another said. It is this affinity that has brought children of survivors together into groups with names like "One Generation After."

Is there a socio-political "syndrome" among the children of survivors? Are there distinct socio-political responses to the Holocaust, if not from all children, then from large segments of them? If there is a syndrome of some kind, and it is too early to say as of new because of lack of research, then it will consist of two major components, each component containing two parts: (1) Particularistic (or Jewish involvement) (a) Religious, (b) Political, and, (2) Universalistic (or beyond the Jewish realm) (a) Religious, (b) Political.

Let us first examine some examples of the particularisticly Jewish ways of confronting the Holocaust. A good number of survivor-children are involved in some form of Jewish commitment. This commitment is based on the idea that young Jews feel they must not give Hitler a posthumous "victory;" that is, they must not assimilate and disappear as Jews, thus giving Hitler his ultimate triumph -- the annihilation of the Jewish people. These young Jews become survivalists, and in defiance of anti-Semitic abuse, they emerge as "new" Jews, fighting-proud Jews. Religiously, this can lead to Orthodox or Hasidic life styles; politically to a variety of expressions ranging from a tough chauvinistic stance like the Jewish Defense League or the right-wing Revisionist Zionist position of youth groups like Betar, to a tough socialist, leftist position.

It can include being Jewish activists; being involved in the rights of Soviet Jews; editing Jewish magazines; organizing religious communal groups; and other similar pursuits. Israel becomes important as the visible continuity of Jewish survival. These interests are of course effected by similar parental political activity and by Jewish education in Hebrew schools, but can also emerge from other sources; the direct immersion in Holocaust literature, a visit to Israel and its Holocaust centers (Yad Vashem or Kibbutz Yad Mordechai, for example), or a particular writer or teacher, such as Elie Weisel or Emil Fackenheim. In the past ten years, whenever Israel was threatened, the nightmare of another Holocaust re-appeared and this too has led to increased political activity on the part of Holocaust survivors and their children.

In the universalistic setting beyond the Jewish realm, young Jews would see in the Holocaust a motif for present-day political concerns -- nuclear Holocaust, the Vietnam war, racism, air and water pollution, and violence. Jewish universalists have found a Jewish setting for their activities too narrow and confining. Therefore, they would go beyond Judaism to embrace other elements. Religiously, this could include a millenial religious movement or cult in which they could work not only for the salvation of the Jews but for all people. It would be interesting to find out how many children of survivors have joined such cults. In all likelihood the number is small because such a non-Jewish cult would be a negation of their Jewish identity which the Holocaust etched so sharply, yet some young Jews would opt for this alternative despite the anguished reaction of parents and friends.

More likely, Holocaust survivor-children will be involved in universal <u>political</u> movements, either radical groups such as socialist or Marxist sects or liberal groups working in the area of human rights, ecology, nuclear energy, and race relations. The image of the Holocaust is powerful and while not the only factor, it is an important one in understanding why and how some children react to their parents' experience by joining radical or liberal political movements.

Is There a Survivor Syndrome?
A Conclusion of Sorts

What can be said in summary? First, with regard to the presence of a psychological survivor syndrome among first generation parents of the Holocaust, the evidence for its existence is overwhelming. The works of Winnik, Krystal, Neiderland and others, plus the compendium of literature on the subject of Krystal and Niederland, (1971) confirms this conclusion. It should be emphasized that most survivors have adapted to their trauma quite well, and more stress should be placed on the positive side of this adaptation. Furthermore, more research is needed on the social psychology and the sociology of survivors and of survivor communities in the world. Too often, psychiatrists have emphasized the pathological and they have done so using clinical samples that are too small and unrepresentative of the range of adaptations and coping mechanisms that survivors utilize.

As for a socio-political syndrome, the evidence shows that there does appear to be a constellation of adaptive mechanisms at work -- conservatism, traditionalism, political paranoia, concern for Israel, but more research is needed to confirm the range of this syndrome politically, sociologically, and religiously.

As for the children of survivors, there exist some problems with generalizations. Some scholars feel that it is too early to report about the exact specificity of a psychological syndrome or its absence (Kestenberg, 1972). A good deal of research is being undertaken now and some reliable answers should be available soon. There is a basis for a secondary guilt syndrome emerging in the children of survivors; a second-generation syndrome may emerge. It will likely be mild in its psycho-pathological aspects, but there will be some exceptions, as Kestenberg herself discovered. One should not exaggerate the severity of such a syndrome; most children of survivors are the normal everyday neurotics that one finds among any highly educated group.

Regarding a socio-political syndrome among the children of survivors, again there may well be not just one syndrome or constellation of responses, but several kinds, either religious or political and either universal or particular. The offspring of Holocaust survivors have to mold some kind of response and find some form of meaning to their experience, and this can lead to a fascinating and diverse set of reactions. Naturally, the Holocaust is not the only independent variable affecting one's social, political, or religious life. Other variables such as one's secular and religious education, childhood relationships with parents, political and cultural socialization, the politics of one's parents, and related factors, aside from the Holocaust, are clearly crucial. What is certain is that a small but significant number of the children of survivors have a fascination for revolutionary, radical, or millenial movements and this fact in itself is a significant observation worthy of future research.

The cycle continues. The second generation is getting married and having children. Some of these children are already in their early teens. Most of the third generation survivors' (grand) children are young. It is still too early to predict about a syndrome on their part. There should be no psychological syndrome of any consequences unless the parents have serious psychological problems directly related to their parents' Holocaust experience. But as for a socio-political syndrome, it would not be surprising if particular traditions related to the Holocaust are passed on to future generations. Just as the Daughters of the American Revolution continue to adhere to a tradition many generations later, so too there may well be socio-political and religious responses specifically developed by the offspring of survivors, trailing far into the future.

Funding for this research came from the Wein Foundation of Chicago under the direction of Dr. Byron Sherwin of Spertus College. This article is a greatly expanded version of a paper which appeared in the anthology, Encountering the Holocaust, edited by Byron Sherwin and Susan Ament (Impact Press/Hebrew Publishing Co., 1979). Reprint permission from Byron Sherwin (Ed.). An earlier version of this paper was read at the Second International Victimology Conference, held at Northeastern University in Boston, in September 1976. Thanks to Dr. Robert Ravven and the staff of the Countway Medical Library of Harvard University for their support and assistance.

1981

References

Epstein, H. The heirs of the holocaust. The New York Times Magazine, June 19, 1977, 12-15; 74-77.

Fogelman, E. and Savran, B. Therapeutic groups for children of holocaust survivors. International Journal of Group Psychotherapy, 1979, 29(2), 211-236.

Greenblatt, S. The influence of survival guilt in chronic family crises. Journal of Psychology and Judaism, 1978, 2(2), 19-28.

Grosser, G., Welchsler, H., and Greenblatt, M. (Eds.). The threat of impending disaster: Contributions to the psychology of distress. Cambridge, Mass., MIT Press, 1964.

Kestenberg, J. Psychoanalytic contributions to the problem of children of survivors from Nazi persecutions. Israel Annals of Psychiatry and Related Disciplies, 1972, 10(4), 311-325.

Krystal, H. and Niederland, W. (Eds.). Psychic trauma tization. Boston: Little, Brown, 1971.

Mostysser, T. Children of survivors: Growing up in America with a holocaust heritage. Martyrdom and Resistance, 1975, 1(6), 4-5.

Sigal, J. Second-generation effects of massive psychic trauma. In H. Krystal and Wm. Niederland (Eds.), Psychic traumatization. Boston: Little, Brown, 1971.

CAN ENEMIES BECOME FRIENDS?
UKRAINIAN-JEWISH RELATIONS TODAY

Can bitter enemies like Ukrainians, Poles, and Lithuanians become friends of Jews today? Can dialogue and even friendship develop among these groups? These are questions that I grapple with. My tentative answer is affirmative -- up to a point. Some steps have been taken quietly in several cities already. Nevertheless, there are Jews who will never be a party to such dialogues, and there will be Ukrainians, Poles, and others who will never stop hating Jews, but small, quavering steps are being taken, if nothing else than, to educate the younger generations. This essay will describe several such dialogues amidst the genesis of historical conflict.

The American Jewish Committee (AJC) has organized a Polish-Jewish desk in its New York office on ethnic pluralism and several meetings have been held in the past few years. A wonderful photography display on the Warsaw Ghetto was shown to critical acclaim in New York City by a non-Jewish Pole. The AJC's Philadelphia chapter has spearheaded efforts to develop closer contacts and mutual understanding with Christians of Ukrainian descent. Rabbi Marc Tannenbaum, national director of the AJC's department of interreligious affairs, and chapter leaders Mrs. Ruth Septee and Seymour Piwoz met with Metropolitan Stephen Sulyk, the highest ranking Ukrainian Catholic prelate in the U.S., and Ukrainian Catholic lay leaders, including Dr. Richard Hanusey. This meeting, hailed as a "first" of its kind, was intended to reduce tensions between the two communities ever a naturalization trial against a Ukrainian-born resident of Philadelphia, an alleged Nazi war criminal and collaborator. The AJC chapter hopes to follow-up this meeting with joint cultural and scholarly activities.

The National Conference of Christians and Jews has also been involved with programming in order to bring together Eastern European ethnic groups like Poles, Ukrainians, and Latvians with Jews. Genesis 2, a Boston-based newspaper, has published an open letter from Poland (November 1980 issue) discussing the "misrepresentation" of the image of Poles in Nazi-occupied areas. The letter, written by a young Polish couple, one of whom is Jewish, is long and impassioned yet wonderfully documented with books and articles on the Holocaust written by Polish writers, and presents a very different view, a Polish viewpoint that says that Poles too suffered and died under the brutal Nazi regime. In the very next issue of Genesis 2 (December 1980), Sam Weintraub, a writer from Boston, responds in a letter called "Polish Anti-Semitism: Sterotype or Reality?" where he questions the accuracy of the Polish letter and is deeply upset about the "grossly incorrect historical information" and the "insensitivity and subtle anti-Semitism which the authors betray in their apology for the inaction of Poles in the face of Jewish suffering".

I myself have also been involved in a small way with Ukrainian-Jewish dialogue. I have lectured on Ukrainian-Jewish partisans at the Ukrainian Research Institute at Harvard University and have been in correspondence with several young Ukrainian scholars, especially Dr. Bohdan Wytwycky of New Jersey and Professor Frank Sysyn of Boston. I have also tried to convince leaders in the Struggle for Soviet Jewry to make alliances with Ukrainian and other ethnic groups who desire religious and political freedom, especially the case of Ukrainian historian and dissident Valentyn Moroz. (Moroz has been freed and lives in Toronto, but there are others).

The reception of my talk at Harvard was good even though the audience was small and contained few Ukrainians. One young man, almost with tears in his eyes, pleaded that I must understand how the Ukrainians also suffered and how some even saved Jewish lives. I was moved by the sincerity of the man and in examining several works by Philip Friedman and Bohdan Wytwycky I have come to the conclusion that there indeed were Ukrainians who both saved Jewish lives and who suffered greatly. There were as Wytwycky notes, "many circles of hell", while the Jewish circle of course was the worst of all.

* * * *

Why now? Why this sudden interest in dialogue between former enemies? First, there is the distance from the tragic events. This is especially true for the second generation, the children of survivors. This second generation of Jews, Ukrainians, Poles, Latvians, and Germans want to know what their parents and grandparents tried to repress or forget. This younger generation is not as emotionally tied to the traumas of the war and is able to put away the old hatreds and memories and start anew. Furthermore, there is less anti-Slavic prejudice among second-generation Jews. The impact of the NBC Holocaust television series also heightened awareness not only among Jews but among younger Eastern Europeans as well.

Perhaps, too, today's Jews and Ukrainians, Poles, Latvians, and others have a common enemy -- Soviet Communism -- which wishes to erase and demolish ethnic and religious identity. As Professor Frank Sysyn of the Harvard Ukrainian Research Institute puts it: why does the American educational system, press, and public stubbornly continue to view all Soviet citizens as Russians and the country as Russia? Part of the problem is historical. The Russian Empire of the 19th Century included most of the areas now in the Soviet Union -- therefore the USSR is viewed merely as a transformed Russia. Since the Tsarist state was created from a Russian core and esposed a Russian nationalist ideology, Americans overlook the existence of non-Russians. With little historical perspective, Americans view Central Asia, the Causasus, the Baltic area, and Ukraine as always naturally having been part of Russia. They forget, Sysyn insists, that most of these areas were annexed, forcibly, to the Russian state only since the 18th century. Such ignorance and mis-information leads some people to talk about "Kiev, Russia" or "Russian dancers from Vilnius", and terribly offends the dignity of a substantial number of Americans of Armenian, Belorussian, Estonian, Latvian, Lithuanian, Rumanian-Moldavian, and Ukrainian descent. Just as Russian Jews have spearheaded the drive for freedom in the Soviet Union, so to have many of the above groups, and it is too bad that there is so little cooperation between Jews and these groups in the struggle against Soviet oppression.

Part of the problem is historical. Jews see most of these groups as their enemies, not only from the Nazi period, but even earlier, back to the days of Bohdan Khmelnitsky, an infamous name to Jews but a revered hero to Ukrainians, but more over, Khmelnitsky, too, is a pawn in Soviet propaganda. The reason there are so many statues to him in Ukraine is that he signed the 1654 Pereiaslav Treaty in which Ukraine and Russia became allies. This treaty has been used by the Russians as a pretext to dominate Ukraine. As Ukrainian scholar Bohdan Wytwytcky emphasizes: Given the role that Russian chauvinism plays in internal Soviet policies, it is not surprising that Khmelnitsky is revered officially. But to blame Ukrainians for this and for concealing the site of Babi Yar and not building a memorial there until relatively recently is unfair. Ukrainians qua Ukrainians did not and still do not have the prerogative of making such decisions. They are made by the central Soviet authoritites, not the Ukrainians.

* * * *

Wytwycky, in a seminal essay entitiled "The Specter of the Holocaust," notes that it is indisputable that the history of Jewish-Ukrainian relations have been marked by friction and conflict. But this should not be surprising given that these two peoples inhabited the same territory, frequently possessed incompatible interests, and lived in a land which has seen more than its share of famine, revolution, war, civil war, and anarchy. It is also indisputable that there has been anti-Semitism among Ukrainians. Wytwycky, however, makes a convincing argument that Ukrainians are not particularly more anti-Semitic than other nations and furthermore, their hostilities toward Jews are not derived solely because of anti-Semitism but are due to other causes.

Most Ukrainians in the 17th century were poor peasants enslaved by a system of serfdom whose beneficiaries were Polish lords and princes. In a highly provocative and inevitibly explosive arrangement, Jews served as managers of the estates and, as tax collectors. Not surprisingly, Wytwycky notes, the daily fare of oppression, exploitation, and humiliation which the Ukrainian serfs had to endure caused the build-up of tremendous resentment which, when opportunity arose, spilled over into rage and rebellion. When this happened, as it did at the time of Khmelnitsky and the Cossack uprising retribution was fierce. The rampaging peasants slaughtered Poles, Jews, and Ukrainians who were in the service of or aligned with the Polish nobility. There were terrible pogroms and they are inexcusable but were they only the product of anti-Semitism? Or was the entire fabric of social, political, and economic life part of the problem? In short, a deeper understanding of the conditions leading to Ukrainian-Jewish conflicts can help us go beyond the Sunday school myths that we all grew up with. Most importantly, it can hopefully lead to the beginnings of a dialogue and perhaps, to bonds of friendship between Jews and Ukrainians.

* * * *

The Holocaust was another testing ground for these
relations. Philip Friedman, one of the few Jewish historians who has examined objectively Ukrainian-Jewish
relations during the Nazi occupation, emphasized (in
1958) that past relations were marked by social tension
and conflicts. Although both parties were oppressed by
the same ruling nations (whether Polish, Russian, or
German), there did not arise a desire for common soli-
darity against their oppressors. This is the sad note
in their intertwined histories. From around the 16th
century, for reasons stated above, Jews were massacred
by Ukrainian peasants and Cossacks in 1648-49 (in the
time of Bohdan Khmelnitsky), in 1768 (the Haidamaks),
and in 1918-1921 (in the time of Simon Petlura). These
events had a powerful effect upon Ukrainian-Jewish
relations in the 20th century, especially during the
Nazi period. And it was exacerbated by the assassination of Petlura on May 25, 1926 by a Ukrainian Jew,
Sholem Schwartzbart. Most Jews felt that Petlura was
responsible for the pogroms of 1918-1921; but the
Ukrainians, both the extreme nationalists as well as
the democratic and liberal elements, regarded Petlura
as a national hero and martyr, and totally denied his
complicity in the pogroms. Nevertheless, this act
would remain in the minds of many Ukrainians, adding
fuel to anti-Jewish and anti-Bolshevik propaganda that
would appear during the next two tumultuous decades.

Friedman, however, does mention the positive
moments in Ukrainian-Jewish relations. Although contacts between the Ukrainian and Jewish intellectual
strata were few, the relations between the Ukrainian
and Jewish masses -- with the above noted exceptions --
were generally friendly. This amicable rapport is
reflected in the mutual influences of Ukrainian and
Jewish folklore, folksongs, melodies, as well as in the
great spiritual movement of Hassidism. Friedman goes
on to mention several Jews who rose to prominence in
the Ukrainian national movement and the Ukrainian
literary renaissance in the 20th century as well as
various political alliances and friendships. But these
were to be short-lived. The influence of UNDO (Ukrainian Nationalists, founded in 1929) was in the ascen-
dant. The Ukrainians were in a mood of utter despair
and disillusionment between the wars as in independent
Ukraine collapsed under the blows of Polish and Soviet
armies. The nationalist OUN, itself to split into a
moderate wing under Colonel Andrew Melnyk, and an

extremist group under Stephan Bandera, son of a Ukrainian priest and a leader of the OUN in Galicia. It was Bandera's groups (called Banderivtsy) who were to pose such a danger to Jewish, Russian, Polish, and Ukrainian Communist and anti-fascist partisans and civilians. There is not enough space to go into the Holocaust phase of Ukrainian-Jewish relations, but here, too, as Friedman and Wytwycky point out, the picture was not always black and white, with Jews the good guys and Ukrainians the bad guys. There were Ukrainians who risked their lives for Jews and there were Ukrainians who fought the fascists alongside of Jews. There were leaders even as high as the rank of Metropolitan Andreas Sheptytsky, Archbishop of Lviv and titular head of the Ukrainian Greek Catholic Church in Galicia, who boldly condemned both Germans and fellow Ukrainians who collaborated in killing Jews. He himself saved several Jewish rabbis. Sheptytsky lived to see the Nazis crushed and driven from his country. He died soon after Soviet occupation, and a petition was submitted by Archbishop Ivan Buchko for his beautification.

* * * *

In the past, Jewish historians like Philip Friedman and Ukrainian scholars such as Volodymyer Stakhiw have called out for research and publications on Ukrainian-Jewish relations, especially regarding the Nazi period. As Friedman emphasized, there is a wide gulf separating Jewish and Ukrainian interpretations of the issues involved, and the lack of reliable and thorough documentation is certainly no help in narrowing this gap and in bringing closer divergent views of Jewish and Ukrainian scholars. And, I might add, Jewish and Ukrainian laypeople.

But steps are now being taken to rectify this. For the past decade, the Ukrainian Research Institute at Harvard University and similar groups in Canada have quietly engaged American and Israeli scholars, both Jewish and Ukrainian, in research seminars and study sessions. These efforts will, I believe, multiply. Time, a great healer, and curiosity will help. As a son of Jewish partisans in the Ukraine (Volynhia) and as a Jew born in the Ukraine, I have never been able to claim one part of my identity, the Ukrainian, before this time. Perhaps now the search for my roots will help in the struggle for Ukrainians and Jews to meet and talk and explore their common identity. We were both oppressed by the Nazis and we are today both oppressed by the Soviet state. We both suffer the potential loss of memory and destiny through assimilation (either forced as in the Soviet Union) or benign, (as in the USA and Canada). The time is ripe for dialogue.

1982

Selected Readings

Armstrong, John A., Ukrainian Nationalism, New York: Columbia University Press, 1963.

_____, (ed.) Soviet Partisans in World War II, Madison, WI: University of Wisconsin Press, 1964. A massive compendium of articles on anti-Nazi resistance based on primary archival material.

Bartoszewski, Wladyslaw and Zofia Lewin (eds.), Righteous Among Nations: How Poles Helped the Jews 1939-1945, London: Earlscourt, 1969; American edition: The Samaritans: Heroes of the Holocaust, Twayne Publishers, 1970. A massive 834-page version of a Polish book. For a review of the Polish original, see Alexander Donat, "Their Brothers' Polish Keepers", Midstream, April 1968, 69-74.

Bauminger, Arieh L., The Roll of Honor, Jerusalem: Yad Vashem (auspices), 1970. An illustrated, 95-page collection of sketches of 24 case histories of "righteous gentiles" from various countries plus a list of 350 names of those who up to 1969 were awarded the Yad Vashem Medal of Honor. Needs to be updated.

Friedman, Philip, Their Brothers' Keepers, New York: Holocaust Library, 1978. (First published in 1957 by Crown Publishers). An excellent synopsis of various Christian "good samaritans" collected by the renowned Holocaust scholar. Good selections on Ukraine and the Baltics plus useful bibliography.

_____, "Ukrainian-Jewish Relations During the Nazi Occupation", New York: YIVO Annual of Jewish Social Science, 1958-1959, 259-296. Reprinted in Friedman's collected essays, Roads to Extinction, Philadelphia, PA: Jewish Publication Society, 1980. Excellent, balanced treatment.

Goldhagen, Erich, "The Soviet Treatment of the Holocaust", Midstream, Volume 25, No. 10, December 1979, 5-7. The shabby and at times vicious treatment of the Holocaust in Soviet literature.

Hanusiak, Michael, Lest We Forget, Toronto: Progress Books, 1976. A very rare document: a Ukrainian-

American account of Ukrainians who helped massacre Jews, with explicit photographs and documents to prove it.

Iranek-Osmecki, Kazimierz, He Who Saves One Life: A Documented Story of the Poles Who Struggled to Save the Jews During World War II, New York: Crown, 1972.

Kamanetsky, Ihor, Hitler's Occupation of Ukraine 1941-1944, Milwaukee, WI: Marquette University Press, 1956.

_____, Secret Nazi Plans for Eastern Europe, New York: Bookman Associates, 1961.

"Letter from Poland", Genesis 2, November 1980. A Boston Jewish Newspaper. With a response from Sam Weintraub in the December 1980 issue.

Leuner, Heinz David, When Compassion Was a Crime: German Silent Heroes 1933-1945, London: Oswald Wolff, 1966.

Lubachko, Ivan S., Belorussia Under Soviet Rule, 1917-1957, Lexington, KY: University of Kentucky Press, 1972.

Mirchuk, Petro, In the German Mills of Death, 1941-1945, New York: Vantage Press, 1976.

Moroz, Valentyn, Report from the Beria Reserve, Toronto: Peter Martin Associates, 1974. Protest writings of a Ukrainian political prisoner in the USSR, how free and living in Canada.

Porter, Jack Nusan (ed.), Jewish Partisans: A Documentary of Jewish Resistance in the Soviet Union During World War II, Lanham, MD: University Press of America, 1982, two volumes. A collection of first-hand memoirs on the cooperation of Jewish and Russian partisans in their struggle against the SS and Ukrainian nationalists. With photos and maps.

_____, Confronting History and Holocaust: Collected Essays, 1972-1982, Lanham, MD: University Press of America, 1983. Several essays are of interest here, especially the ones dealing with Ukrainian, Russian, and Jewish partisans.

Sysyn, Frank E., "Russia or the Soviet Union?" (pamphlet), Cambridge, MA: Ukrainian Research Institute, Harvard University, n.d. (1982).

Wytwycky, Bohdan, The Other Holocaust: Many Circles of Hell, Washington, DC: The Novak Report, 1980. A useful essay that tries to present the "other side", the side of Ukrainians and other Slavs who were to be marked for extermination by slave labor as soon as the Jewish "problem" was solved. A refreshingly new angle on the Holocaust by a compassionate young Ukrainian scholar.

NEO-NAZIS IN THE USA: AN INTERVIEW

by Art Jahnke

Sociologist and author Dr. Jack Nusan Porter lost twenty-five relatives, including two sisters, to the Nazi during World War II. The son of a Jewish commander of partisan forces in the Ukraine, Porter has spent the last two years studying the neo-Nazi movement in the United States. Porter's research was funded by the Memorial Foundation for Jewish Culture, which is largely financed by the money from German reparations.

First of all, how many Nazis are there in the United States?

The total of hard-core members in the United States is probaly not more than 500. Altogether there are maybe 2000.

Why should anyone worry about a few hundred crazies?

Well, it's true that they attract only very few people, but enough that they can cause mischief, especially if they get into terrorism, as they have in Europe. And when they start running for office, as they already have here, you have to educate people about the Holocaust and fascism. Hitler started with just a few motorcycle bums, a few disgruntled army veterans, and a country that, like ours, had been economically weakened and lacked strong leadership. So if a depression hits this country, we better get worried.

How old is the Nazi movement in this country?

There are two Nazi parties. One is called the Ausland, which is the overseas branch of the German Nazis. Until the end of World War II they were fairly strong. I found in my reserch that the connection between these Nazis and the Ku Klux Klan goes back to the thirties. I have a photograph of a Ku Klux Klanner and a German Bund Nazi in a rally in the late thirties.

After World War II the movement went into decline and was resurrected almost single-handedly by George Lincoln Rockwell. He build them up to a few thousand before he was assassinated by another Nazi.

We never hear anything about a Nazi party in this country. What names do the Nazis go by?

The big one is the National Socialist White People's Party, and there is also the National Socialist Defense Force. The key words are National Socialist. There is even a gay Nazi group called the National Socialist League.

Which of those groups do we have in New England?

There isn't too much in Boston, but Providence, Rhode Island, has a very active neo-Nazi group and they do something really terrible. If somebody who is Jewish dies, they will send a sympathy letter signed the Nazi party. They also send out Christmas and Hanukka cards. They like to get Jews uptight. They use Jews, and they use the Left to get people to attack them. They are very happy to have 3000 people attack them.

How do the Nazis go about legitimizing such racist ideology as theirs?

Racist theories are legitimized by many people in the public eye. I'm very upset right now with Noam Chomsky, who is a Jew and a leftist. Chomsky wrote the preface to a book by a French historian, Robert Flaurisson, who claims that the Nazi gas chambers never existed and that facts about the Holocaust have been greatly exaggerated. Flaurisson was even dismissed from his post as a professor at the University of Lyons in the wake of a scandal caused by the book. Chomsky does state that he doesn't share Flaurisson's views, but he favors freedom of expression.

What kind of people are attracted to the Nazi parties?

The Nazis attract a lot of young people, and I mean even fourteen- and fifteen-year-old kids. They attract the embittered, the unemployed, plus a few eccentric upper-class intellectuals. They also get a lot of bikers. Bikers seem to like all the Nazis regalia. In fact, one of the problems the Nazis have is that they can't seem to attract a better class of person.

Apply this to a larger scale and you see that the social and economic reasons that Reagan came to power also explain the rise of the neo-Nazis and the Klan. High unemployment, economic problems, a vacuum in leadership, a sense that the welfare state is one gray

mass. People don't want to be part of that. They want
to do something that will change the world.

Speaking of changing the world, what can you tell us
about John Hinckley?

Hinckley was a member of the National Socialist White
People's party for a while, but he was too radical for
them. If you're too radical for them you're either an
FBI agent, a provocateur, or just a crazy nut.

What kind of counter-Nazi forces do the Nazis have to
worry about?

There are people who work very quietly trying to eliminate Nazis. Some of them are Jews and some are not.
Some assassinate them. Some use blackmail and some use
bombs. There are alot of crazy people out there.

In the last year we've had at least two Nazis run for
political office, and we've seen the desecration of
synagogues on Long Island, New York. Are the Nazi
growing in ranks or are they just growing bolder?

There really hasn't been much increase in numbers in
the last five years, but they are becoming more respec-
table. When they can take off their uniforms and get
in a suit and run for office, this is a very dangerous
situation. They are pulling the wool over people's
eyes. The Moral Majority has some good points, about
family and other things, and the Nazis say some good
things, too. They want to end unemployment, too -- but
beneath all that is genocide.

1981

-118-

WHAT HAPPENS WHEN NAZIS ARE ELECTED TO U.S. OFFICE?

The marathon television production, "Holocaust," which began on NBC Sunday night and continues through Wednesday for a total of nine and one-half hours, brings back the horrors of Hitler's Germany. The vivid reminder of those dark years makes all the more repugnant the prospect of Thursday's full-scale Nazi Party parade in Skokie, Illinois, a predominantly Jewish Chicago suburb whose residents include some 7,000 concentration camp survivors.

With the help of the American Civil Liberties Union, the party has won a series of court battles over its right to march in Skokie on April 20, the anniversary of the Fuehrer's birth. The final obstacle was removed last month when federal judge overturned a local ordinance that barred the wearing of military style uniforms in public demonstrations.

Although the marchers' goal is to rally support for what they see as a growing popular movement, these fanatics really pose no major threat to the United States. Organized into a dozen or so groups, their membership numbers no more than 2,000, though their sympathizers easily add up to 200 times that figure.

The largest group is the National Socialist White People's Party, which claims some 400 members nationwide. Others include the National Socialist Liberation Front of Los Angeles, the National Socialist League in Los Angeles and San Francisco, the National Socialist Movement in Cincinnati, the White Power Movement (founded in West Virginia by German-born George Dietz) and even one in Nebraska calling itself the overseas branch of the German Workers' National Socialist Party.

While American Nazis and other openly racist groups have staged marches and rallies in the past, they have only recently begun to enter electoral politics. Their candidates have been on the ballot for school boards in a handful of major cities, have run for alderman in Chicago and for mayor in Milwaukee and Houston. An avowed white-supremacist anti-Semite has even entered primary elections for governor and lieutenant governor of Georgia.

None of these candidates have won election so far, but Jesse Stoner, whose platform called for eradication of Jews and blacks, amassed 71,000 votes in 1974, when he came in fourth in a field of 10 candidates in the Georgia lieutenant governor's race. Someday soon, one of his ilk will probably win a local election.

I mention this likelihood because overtly racist groups are growing more sophisticated. They have even begun using the mass media for political campaigns in which they actually advocate genocide. Given this state of affairs, two ways of handling the problem suggest themselves:

- Congress could simply outlaw groups that espouse the annihilation of a people. The Potsdam treaty, to which the United States is a signatory, could provide a legal precedent. (That post-World War II agreement required participating nations to outlaw Nazi groups.) However, because it is widely believed that Potsdam regulations do not extend to neo-Nazis --that is, groups that did not spring from pre-war German activity -- it is unlikely that such a law would ever hold up in court.

- Courts could limit Nazis free speech rights to particular times and places. While the First Amendment ensures free speech and expression, judges have held that such a right is not absolute. For example, words which, by their very utterance, inflict injury or tend to incite a breach of the peace are not protected. Society's right to maintain public order outweighs the right to speak them.

Though many believe that Skokie's plight calls for government-imposed restraint on potentially provocative speech, the courts have disagreed. If Jewish groups approach Nazism as a free speech issue, they will lose their case, for the courts will reluctantly continue to support Nazi rights, the ACLU will reluctantly continue to defend those rights -- and the Nazis will continue to march onward.

But what will the majority of Americans do when Nazis and other hate groups win office and try to act on their bizarre ideologies? At that point, how will the ACLU react?

I see only one way to put the brakes on Nazi hatemongers: through education about the horrors of racism. I propose educating all Americans through every conceivable means, from movies and documentaries to classroom courses and fictionalized TV specials, such as NBC's current series.

Some steps have been taken to establish Holocaust studies in public schools. Last year, the National Council for the Social Studies and the Anti-Defamation League of B'nai B'rith cosponsored a conference on genocide and the Holocaust to which educators thronged from all over the United States and abroad. Partly as a result of the conference, some schools have already incorporated Holocaust courses in their curricula.

In Brookline, Massachusetts, classes are offered in the eighth grade, while Philadelphia, Milwaukee and New York plan to initiate high school courses. As scores of other cities express interest, a spokesman for the Department of Health, Education and Welfare has pledged federal support for teaching about genocide in general and the Holocaust in particular.

The current groundswell of interest in Holocaust studies is heartening, for in the long run educating each and every American about its atrocities is the only way to win the war against ignorance and hate.

1978

THE AFFIRMATION OF LIFE AFTER THE HOLOCAUST:
THE CONTRIBUTIONS OF BETTELHEIM, LIFTON, AND FRANKL

Too often what emerges after studying or reading about the Holocaust is a debased image of man and woman. However, in examining the works of certain psychologists, what we find is just the opposite: the affirmation of life. The goal of this short essay is to present a brief synopsis of the major contributions of three psychotherapists regarding the lessons to be learned from the Holocaust.

These three men are perhaps the three best known figures in this field (aside from Erich Fromm): Viennese psychiatrist Viktor E. Frankl (author of Man's Search for Meaning: An Introduction to Logotherapy); University of Chicago psychiatrist Bruno Bettelheim (author of The Informed Heart: Autonomy in a Mass Age); and Yale psychiatrist Robert Jay Lifton (author of Death in Life: Survivors of Hiroshima; History and Human Survival, and with Eric Olsen, Living and Dying).[1]

These three men have confronted the "unthinkable" while forcing their readers to confront the evil in men. All three have not only confronted but transcended it with a psychologically and politically healthier vision of the future.

Bettelheim and Frankl are both European Jews who not only survived World War II but personally experienced the concentration camps themselves. Lifton, a much younger man and an American Jew, derived his lessons not from the Nazi Holocaust alone, but from intense interviews with survivors of the first A-bomb blast in Hiroshima. Of the three, only Frankl has developed the most comprehensive theory and method -- existential therapy or logotherapy. Logotherapy emerged in Frankl's mind as he was struggling to survive in a death camp where his father, mother, brother, and wife had died. With every possession gone, every value destroyed, everyone close to him dead, cold, hungry or brutalized, how could he not merely survive but continue to find meaning in life?[2]

He survived the camps with the same techniques that he later used in therapy with patients. He found meaning in life through several ways -- by conjuring up happy images of his wife and family, by interviewing

camp inmates and gathering material for his future
book, and by controlling his thoughts in an institution
that hoped to control not only bodies but minds.

Bettelheim did the same though his camp conditions
were much more comfortable than Frankl's. Both survived because they strove for "autonomy in a mass age".
In a world that had gone beyond the wildest fantasies
of Orwell's 1984 and Aldous Huxley's Brave New World,
they and Lifton hope to teach others what integrity and
hope mean in a world that either pleasurably or pain-
fully takes away freedoms and infiltrates minds with
both trivia and perversions.

While Freud stressed frustration in our sexual
life, Frankl stressed frustration in our will-to-
meaning. To Frankl, our neuroses are existential in
nature; they are caused by an estrangement from life
and an inability to find a full and satisfying meaning
in life. For Frankl, love and suffering are solution.
As he put it, "the crowning experience of all ... is
the wonderful feeling that, after all (man) has suffered, there is nothing he need fear anymore -- except
his God."[3] For Frankl, the final destination of
psychological health is a closeness to man and a
reverence for God. More than either Lifton and
Bettelheim, Frankl's ideas are a very religious
psychiatric experience.

Bettelheim shares Frankl's ultimate vision of
inner-directed autonomy in the face of over-powering
technology and dehumanized bureaucracy, but his theory
of survival lacks an inner coherence and is, in many
ways, more vague. His experiences at Dachau and
Buchenwald led him to two conclusions.[4]

This first conclusion is that psychoanalysis was by
no means the most effective way to change personality.
Being placed in a particular type of environment could
produce much more radical changes and in a much shorter
time. The environment could produce much more radical
changes and in a much shorter time. The environment
can be a negative or positive one. A concentration
camp or prison can produce pathological behavior; a
warm and happy setting can reduce psychopathology. In
a sense, Bettelheim presaged Abraham Maslow, who also
talked about growth-inducing environments. What Maslow
called self-actualization, joy, and creativity can be
stimulated by such environments while neuroses will
develop within settings where the individual was not

living up to his/her potential and where the surroundings were not conducive to growth. Bettelheim, later at the University of Chicago, would apply this insight to his school for emotionally disturbed children, the Sonia Shankman Orthogenic School.

Bettelheim's second conclusion posited the inadequacy of psychoanalytical theory; that it was unable to fully explain what had happened to him and other prisoners. It gave little guidance for understanding what is meant by the "good" life or the "good" person. Psychoanalysis had its limitations: within the appropriate frame of reference, it is clarified much but applied to phenomena outside its province, it was not only inadequate but distorted meaning as well.

Rather than reject psychotherapy entirely, Bettelheim attempted to build an environment of love for his children, an environment where the "heart would be informed with reason" (hence the title of his book) while reason would be invaded by a daring heart. It is this symbiotic symmetry which should be the goal of humanity.

Bettelheim furthermore felt that the oppressive state of Hitler's Germany was a passing phenomenon. In fact he saw it as a challenge and a temporary setback to people's ingenuity. He hoped that this challenge would force people to reach a "higher integration and a deeper consciousness of freedom." His final statement is one of hope, but not false hope. The struggle for mastering the new conditions set by the atomic age will tax all our mental and moral powers if we do not want a "brave new world but an age of reason and humanity."[5]

Robert Jay Lifton continued the work of Frankl and Bettelheim, lifting their vision to higher and higher planes. Unlike his elderly mentors, Lifton did not personally experience the Holocaust; in fact, his theoretical perspective is informed not by the destruction of the Jews in Europe but by two other phenomena: the Japanese survivors of the atomic bomb dropped on Hiroshima and Nagasaki and the returning veterans of the Vietnam War. His writings almost beg inclusion of the Jewish survivors of genocide. While he is aware of the role they play in his theory and while he uses examples of their plight, I am surprised at how few references there are to Jewish concerns in his work. In any case, this does not weaken his case. It only leaves it open to others (including the present writer) to apply his paradigm to the Jewish condition. Lifton has elevated the concept of survivor to include all of us. He has elevated the discussion of death and destruction to monumental psycho-historical heights, and in the process has made it possible for those who are not direct survivors or who have not directly experienced the Holocaust to gain access to the meaning of meaningless death. All of his books have led up to the one book, upon which I shall rely to present to the reader his most important contributions: Living and Dying, written in collaboration with Eric Olson.

Lifton wants us to understand the inscrutable face of death. He wants us not to turn away or distort death but to face it and to face the meaning of death in our lives. He feels that we have "buried death" the way the Victorians buried sex. In fact, though others have already used the term, Lifton speaks of the "pornography of death". But what makes death even more incomprehensible today is that while in the past destruction had limits, today, mass destruction does not merely destroy; it destroys the very boundaries of destruction! We confront not only our own individual meaningless death but the meaningless death of our entire planet.

Lifton and Olson describe five modes or categories of immortality: biological, creative, theological, natural, and experiential.[6] They are as follows:

Biological immortality is the most common mode. It means that a person lives on through his/her own children in an endless chain. This mode is never entirely biological, but is experienced emotionally and symbolically and transcends one's own biological family to include one's tribe, organization, people, nation, and even species. Furthermore, the sense of biological continuity becomes intermingled with cultural continuity as each generation passes its traditions on to the next. Lifton and Olson call this "biosocial immortality" and its implications for Jewish survivors are profound. Holocaust victims continually talk of the triumph of not only the family or the individual but of the entire Jewish people as having outlived Hitler. The reverse is also shown: Hitler and Nazism not only perished but their names must be "blotted out" from memory and history. When referring to Hitler, Torquemado, or Pharoah, Jews conclude with the Hebrew words, Yismach Shimo ("may his name be erased").

Creative immortality is a second mode, and this too has had a long Jewish tradition. One may feel a sense of immortality through teaching, writing, art-making, repairing, construction, composing, healing, inventing, or through some lasting influence on humanity. In some cases, writing a book or constructing a building may even serve as a substitute for having children. The hundreds of diaries and memoirs written during and after the Holocaust are testimony to this mode of immortality.

Theological immortality is the form most readily thought of when one thinks about immortality. Historically, it has been through religion and religious institutions that people have most self-consciously expressed their aspirations for conquering death and living forever. All religions are faced with the concept of immortality and though each gives assurances of it in different ways, no religion is based on the premise that human life is eternally significant. Judaism however underplayed the image of "afterlife" in its theology by constantly stressing that the "good works" on earth will be its own best reward. The literature of the Holocaust rarely stresses "afterlife". The struggle to survive and be witness here and now, rather than later, has been the key element in survivor accounts except for a few ultra-Orthodox sects. Theological immortality raises the question of religious self-sacrifice. The implication that the Holocaust was part of God's will and that to struggle against the Nazis (who presumably were acting according to God's will) was useless and has been rejected by most Jews.

Lifton's fourth mode of immortality is achieved through continuity with nature, again an ancient form of religious communion. Lifton quotes the Hebrew Bible: "From dust you come and to dust you shall return," and comes away with a striking reflection that this represents a Biblical injunction against pride as well as an expression of confidence that the earth itself does not die. Mankind has always looked to nature for spiritual refreshment and revitalization of the spirit.

Lifton's final mode of immortality is what he calls experiential transcendence. This mode differs from the others in that it depends solely on a psychological state. This state is one of rapture, ecstasy, of being "at one with oneself and with the universe." It can also be a state where one "dies and is reborn." This mode can be found in the search for a theological rebirth, but there are other means: music, song, dance, battle, athletics, sexual love, childbirth, and intense comradship. This experience can occur in relation to the four other modes (biological, creative, theological, natural) or by itself. Over the centuries, humans have used heightened states of consciousness to reach this form of immortality: fasting, drugs, liquor, or combinations of these.

In many societies and religions, including Judaism, experiential transcendence is encouraged through fiestas, carnivals, holidays, and celebrations which help people to break free from the restraint of routine and to sing, dance, drink, laugh, and love in a spirit of excess. The Hippie movement of the middle-to-late sixties was a movement of spiritual transcendence, and even though it was later over-run by hustlers, violent criminals, rip-off artists, and hard drugs, it nevertheless was a movement spawned by the threat of destruction and meaningless. In a recent issue commemorating the 10th anniversary of Haight-Ashbury, the San Francisco center for "hippies", the writer noted the following:

It seemed like a nation gone mad, at war with Asian peasants, with its own black citizens in urban ghettos, and with its own white children. And lurking in the background of any war, for the past 30 years, has been the specter of atomic war and total annihilation. Technology itself was more suspect than for any preceding generation. Along with undreamed of wealth and power, it had created undreamed of potential for evil, and the potential for good was being used in only the drabbest and most cautious ways. Technology had proved a blind alley. The Haight was a pressure cooker of new thought, of a new search for new ways to deal with the dangers of modern society.[7]

Lifton understands this generation well, and would easily understand the young children of Jewish survivors who took part in this anti-death movement of the 1960's and who continue to say a collective "no" but in more quiet ways today. In conclusion, Lifton's greatest contribution to these issues is his description of the impact of such "death imagery" on our society, and

his hope in the ability to affirm life in the face of
death. L'chaim ("to life") may seem to be just another
cliche in Jewish life, but in the works of Frankl,
Bettelheim, and Lifton, and to all the survivors of all
the "Holocausts" from Hiroshima to Auschwitz to Vietnam, it is the single most important affirmation in the
world today.

1980

Notes

[1] See in particular the chapter called "The Survivor" in Lifton's Death in Life: Survivors of Hiroshima and Robert J. Lifton and Eric Olson, Living and Dying.

[2] Frankl. Preface to Man's Search for Meaning, p. viii.

[3] Ibid., p. 148.

[4] Bettelheim. The Informed Heart, pp. 18-19.

[5] Ibid., p. 300.

[6] Lifton and Olsen. Living and Dying, pp. 60-74.

[7] Charles Perry, "From Eternity to Here: What a Long Strange Trip It's Been", Rolling Stone, Feb. 26, 1976 (Issue No. 207), p. 52.

My thanks to Harvard University's Frances Countway Library of Medicine and its staff for opening up their vast resources to me, and to Dr. Robert Ravven of Boston for his encouragement and support. Funding for this research came from a grant by the Wein Foundation of Chicago under the direction of Dr. Byron Sherwin of Spertus College. A much larger version of this paper appeared in an anthology edited by Dr. Sherwin: Encountering the Holocaust: An Interdisciplinary Survey, Chicago: Impact Press, 1979; distributed by Hebrew Publishing Company of New York City).

III. THE SPEECHES AND WRITINGS
OF
JACK NUSAN PORTER

The idea for this came to me after perusing a festschrift for Robert K. Merton, compiled by one of his students. I felt it was important to have all of one's writings in one accessible place. Since I am not as famous as Merton nor have I as many students, I thought I would collate the material myself. The first section contains essays, professional articles, books, and reviews for the past fifteen years, with material on journals and newsletters I have published over the past five. The next section contains major speeches and professional papers delivered, for the most part, at scholarly conferences. They do not include the numerous talks given on college campuses before students and faculty or those given at other community forums.

Books, Articles, Essays, Book Reviews Chronologically

1967

"The Negro, the New Left, and the Hippy Movement," The Milwaukee Organizer, August-September, 1967.

1968-1970

Professional Articles

"Towards a Theory of Middlemanship," Master's Thesis, Northwestern University, 1969.
"The Situational Perspective in Sociology through the Works of W.I. Thomas and Alfred Schutz," Heuristics (journal at Northern Illinois University), 1970, pp. 28-34.

Essays

"Jewish Student Activism," Jewish Currents (New York), Vol. 24, 5, May 1970, 28-34.

Book Reviews

Two Against One: Coalitions in Triads by Theodore Caplow in the American Sociological Review, 35, 1, February 1970, 133-34.

The American Ghetto and Beyond by Peter Rose in the
    American Journal of Sociology, 76, 2, September
    1970, 350-351.
Pentagon Capitalism by Seymour Melman in Congress
    Bi-Weekly, December 25, 1970, 34-36.

1971

Professional Articles

"Student Protest and the Technocratic Society: The
    Case of ROTC," Ph.D. Dissertation, Northwestern
    University, June 1971.
"Selected Readings," annotated bibliography for Guy
    Swanson's book Social Change, New York: Scott,
    Foresman, 1971, 171-179.
"Talking Police Blues: The Dilemmas of the Academic,"
    The Insurgent Sociologist, May 1971 and
    Subterranean Padagogy, 1,2, May 1971, 11-13.
"Black-Jewish Relations," International Review of
    Sociology, 1,2, September 1971, 157-165.

Essays

Book Reviews

The Age of Protest by Walt Anderson and The University
    and Revolution by Gary Weaver and James Weaver in
    Sociological Quarterly, February, 1971.
The American Reading Public by Roger Smith in the
    Subterranean Sociological Newsletter, 5, 2,
    December 1971, 30.

1972

Professional Articles

"Jewish Student Activism" reprinted in Minority
    Problems edited by Arnold and Caroline B. Rose,
    New York: Harper and Row, 1972, 326-331.
"Jewish Militancy---A Mini-Bibliography," Association
    for Jewish Studies Newsletter, Vol. 2, 2, July
    1972, 4.

Essays

"The Jewish Defense League: New Tensions in the Old
Melting Pot," Christianity and Crisis, 32, 6,
April 17, 1972.
"Three Views on the JDL," Jewish Currents, May 1972.
"A Jewish Conservative Backlash?", Commonweal, October
13, 1972, pp. 33-37.
"Jewish Resistance During the Holocaust," (four-part
series), Wisconsin Jewish Chronicle, Dec. 1, Dec.
15, Dec. 22, and Dec. 29, 1972.
"Symposium," Response Magazine, 16, Winter 1972-73.

Book Reviews

The New Jews by James Sleeper and Alan Mintz in Jewish
Social Studies, 34, 1, January 1972.
Take One: A Film Journal in The Journal of Popular
Film, 1, 2, Spring 1972, 143-144.
Academic Gamesmanship by Pierre Van Den Berghe in the
American Journal of Sociology, Vol. 78, Summer
1972.

1973

Books

Jewish Radicalism: A Selected Anthololgy (ed. with
Peter Dreier), New York: Grove Press, 1973.
Student Protest and the Technocratic Society: The Case
of ROTC, Adams Press, Chicago, 1973 (My published
dissertation).

Professional Articles

Essays

"The Elections of 1972 and the Jews," Echad: A Jewish
Journal (Chicago), Vol. 1, January 1973.
"An Open Letter to Rabbi Meir Kahane," Echad, 2,
February 1973.
"Israel Needs a Social, Political, but Peaceful
Revolution," Jewish Liberation News Service, May
1973.
"The Jewish Rebel," The Jewish Spectator, June 1973,
15-17.
"Zalonka: The Story of a Jewish Partisan," Davka: A

Jewish Journal (L.A.), 3, 2, Winter-Spring 1973,
14-20.
"The Death of POW Captain Brudno," in the "My Opinion
Section," Milwaukee Journal, July 17, 1973.
"Jewish Radicalism," Judaica Book News, 4, 1,
Fall-Winter 1973-74.

Book Reviews

The Jewish Family by Benjamin Schlesinger in
Contemporary Sociology, January 1973, 550-552.
Family Matters by Lawrence Fuchs in Contemporary
Sociology, May 1973.

1974

Books

The Study of Society, Guilford, Conn.: Dushkin
Publishing Group, 1974, co-contributor.
Teachers Guide, to above book, author.
Sociology Reader, to accompany above book, co-editor.

Professional Articles

"The Jewish Student: A Comparative Analysis of
Religious and Secular Attitudes," YIVO Annual of
Jewish Social Science, 14, 1974, 297-338.
"A New Course Outline: Sociology in Practice," ASA
Footnotes, 2, 6, August 1974.

Essays

"Paranoia and Politics," Davka (of UCLA), 4, 2, Winter
1974, 25-28.
"Yiddish, Yiddish, Yiddish," Writers Digest, 54, 5, May
1974.
"The Singles Scene Probed," Genesis 2, 5, 6, April
1974.
"The Defunis Case," ORT Newsletter, 25, 1,
September-October 1974.
"The Hawatmeh Affair: The Agony Over Palestinian
Rights," Genesis 2, 6, 1, October 1974.
"The Jewish Writer," Writers Digest, 54, 11, December
1974.
"Letter from the East," Davka, 4, 4, Fall 1974.
"What South Boston Wants," (school busing controversy),
Los Angeles Times, Tuesday, December 1974, edi-
torial page. Reprinted in the Chicago Sun-Times

(December 23, 1974), <u>Detroit Free Press</u> (December 22, 1974) and about ten other nationally known newspapers.

Book Reviews

<u>Marriage and its Alternatives</u> by Lucille Duberman in <u>Sociology: A Review of New Books</u>, 1, 6, April 1974.
<u>Contemporary Judaic Fellowship in Theory and Practice</u> by Jacob Neusner in <u>Jewish Social Studies</u>, January 1974.
<u>Reform is a Verb: Notes on Reform and Reforming Jews</u> by Leonard J. Fein et al in <u>Judaism</u>, 23, 2, Spring 1974, 246-249.
<u>The Jews in the Middle East 1860-1972</u> by Hayyim J. Cohen in <u>Sociology: A Review of New Books</u>, 1, 5, March 1974.
<u>The New Anti-Semitism</u> by Arnold Foster and Benjamin Epstein in <u>Sociology: Reviews of New Books</u>, 2, 2, November-December 1974, 26-27.

1975

Professional Articles

"Jewish Radicalism in Transition" (with Peter Dreier), <u>Society</u>, 12, 2, January-February 1975, 34-43.
"Does Standard Grading Encourage Excessive Competiveness?", <u>Change: The Magazine of Higher Learning</u>, 7, 7, September 1975, 44-46.
"Jewish Singles," <u>Midstream</u>, 21, 10, December 1975, 29-37.

Essays

"d.a. levy: the life, death, and poetry of an american jewboy," <u>Jewish Currents</u>, 29, 1, January 1975, 16-23. Portions reprinted in <u>Yesodot</u>, an Israeli journal.
"Shmuel Parsov's Partisans' Tales," <u>Present Tense</u>, 2, 4, Summer 1975, 10-11.

Book Reviews

<u>Poor Jews</u> ed. by Naomi Levine and Martin Hochbaum in <u>Women's American ORT Newsletter</u>, 25, 3, January-February 1975.
<u>The Jewish Community in America</u> and <u>The Jew in American</u>

Society edited by Marshall Sklare and *The Soviet Treatment of Jews* by Harry G. Shaffer in *Contemporary Sociology*, 4,4,July 1975, 416-417.
Radical Paradoxes: Dilemmas of the American Left 1945-1970 by Peter Clecak in *Change Magazine*, 7, 3, April 1975, 13.

1976

Professional Articles

"Jewish Singles" reprinted in *Jewish Digest*, March 1976, pp. 29-37.
"On Genocide" -- review-essay, *Contemporary Sociology*, 5,4,July 1976, 490-492.

Essays

Bibliographic contribution, "American Radical Zionists" by Chava Katz, *Encyclopedia Judaica*, Jerusalem: Keter-Macmillan, *Yearbook* 1975-1976, pp. 126-133.
"Symposium," *Response Magazine*, 10, 1 (#29), Spring 1976.
"Getting Your Name in Print," *Genesis 2*, 8, 4, December 1976
"Carter's Position on the Middle East," *The Jewish Advocate*, 161, 4, Aug. 5, 1976, 1 and 20.

Book Reviews

Jewish Radicals by William Fishman, *The Journal of Ethnic Studies*, Vol. 4, No. 2, Summer 1976, pp. 113-114.
Growing Up in America by F. and G. Hechinger in *ORT Newsletter*, 26 5, May-June 1976, 4.
We are Your Sons by Robert and Michael Meeropol in *Jewish Bookland*, 31, 2, March 1976, 2.
Out of the Whirlwind: A Reader of Holocaust Literature by Albert Friedlander in *Sociological Analysis* (official journal of the Association for the Sociology of Religion), 1976.
Uri Geller: My Story in *The Beacon* (Boston Mensa), 1, 11, November 1976, 13-14.

Professional Articles

"Does Standard Grading Encourage Excessive
Competitiveness?" reprinted in Gerald Levin, Short
Essays: Models for Composition, New York: Harcourt,
Brace, 1977, 224-233.
"Kids in Cults: Why They Join, Stay, and Leave" (with
Irvin Doress), booklet distributed by the National
Hillel Foundations, Washington, D.C., 1977.
"A Nazi Runs for Mayor," Present Tense, 4, 4, Summer
1977, 27-31.
Abstract of my "The Impact of the Holocaust on Children
of Survivors," Victimology: An International
Journal, 2, 1, Spring 1977, 77-78.
Abstract of my "Social and Psychological Obstacles to
Resistance During Genocide, "Victimology, 2, 1,
Spring 1977, 78.
"Doomsday Cult: A Reply, "The American Sociologist, 12,
4, November 1977, p. 203.

Essays

"The Issue of Breira," Midstream, August-September
1977, 89-91.
"The King of Money Collectors," Genesis 2, 8, 6, May
1977, (with Shlomo Porter).
"The Last of the Big-Time Collectors" reprinted in
Jewish Digest, 23, 2, October 1977, 68-71.

Book Reviews

Rebels and Reformers by Alberta Eiseman in the American
Jewish Historical Quarterly, Vol. 66, 3, March
1977, 455-456.
Community and Polity: The Organizational Dynamics of
American Jewry by Daniel Elazar in ORT Reporter,
March-April 1977, Vol. 27, 4.
Ethnic Integration in Israel by Michael Inbar and Chaim
Adler in ORT Reporter (50th Anniversary Issue), 28,
2, November 1977, 4, 14.
Synagogue Life: A Study in Symbolic Interaction by
Samuel C. Heilman in Contemporary Sociology: A
Journal of Reviews, 6, 6, November 1977, p. 740.
Why They Give: American Jews and Their Philanthropies
by Milton Goldin and A Host at Last (The Story of
Brandeis University) by Abram L. Sachar in Jewish
Frontier, 44, 7, August-September 1977, 24-25.

Professional Articles

"The Sociology of Jewry: Blueprints for the Future from
Contemporary Designs," Contemporary Jewry, Vol. 4,
No. 1, Fall-Winter 1977-1978, 24-29.
"A Nazi Runs for Mayor" and "Mr. Goldberg and John
Henry: The Relationship between Afro-American and
American Jews" in J. N. Porter (ed.) The Sociology
of American Jewry, 1978.
"Kids in Cults" (with Irvin Doress), Society, Vol. 15,
No. 4, May-June 1978 (#114), 69-71.
"Rosa Sonnenschein and THE AMERICAN JEWESS: The First
Independent English Language Jewish Women's Journal
in the United States," American Jewish History,
Vol. LXVIII, No. 1, September 1978, 57-63.
"Jewish Women in the Resistance," ORT Reporter,
November-December 1978, 7-8.

Essays

"Psychotherapy and Writing," Modus Operandi (a writers'
journal), March 1978, 5-6.
"Resistance: Ordinary People with Strong Ideology" (on
Jewish Resistance During the Nazi Period), Genesis
2, March 1978, 6, 13.
"Israel: A Retrospective," Genesis 2, special issue on
Israel's 30th Anniversary, April 1978.
"What Happens When Nazis Are Elected to US Office?,"
Los Angeles Times, Monday, April 17, 1978, Op-ed
page.
"Introduction" to M.S. Rosenberg, Quotations for the
Aquarian Age, Seacaucus, N.J.: Citadel Press (Lyle
Stuart, Inc.), 1978.
"Personal History," Modus Operandi (a writers journal),
August 1978.
"Many Jewish Professors at Moon's Conference in
Boston," Jewish Advocate, Dec. 1, 1978, pp. 1 and
24.

---

*Explosion of interest in cults; I appeared on Channel
5 (Good Morning Show); Channel 7 (Mass Reaction, with
Ted O'Brien); and radio shows; also see Boston Globe,
Nov. 23, 1978, p. 17; Boston Herald, Sunday, Nov. 26,
1978; Lowell Sun, Sunday, Nov. 26, 1978. This was in
the wake of the Jonestown, Guyana massacre on Nov. 21,
1978.

Book Reviews

The Survivor by Terrence Des Pres in Jewish Currents,
Vol. 32, No. 4 (#351), April 1978, 32-35.
Freud, Jews, and Other Germans by Peter Gay, in JWB
Books in Review (JWB Circle), Vol. XXXIV, No. 5,
November 1978, 22.
A Coat of Many Colors: Jewish Subcommunities in the
U.S. by Abraham D. Lavender in Contemporary
Sociology, Vol. 7, No. 6, November 1978, 788-789.

Books

The Sociology of American Jews: A Critical Anthology,
University Press of America, (4710 Auth Place,
Washington, D.C. 20023 South East), $8.25.
The Journal of the History of Sociology, Vol. 1, No. 1,
November 1978. First issue came out, edited by
Jack Nusan Porter and Glenn Jacobs.
Research Monographs and Prospectuses
"Collective Disorders," co-author of prospectus for
Contract Research Corporation, Belmont, Mass., June
1978, for United States Department of Justice, Law
Enforcement Assistance Administration (LEAA),
Washington, D.C. 20531
"On the Holocaust," see the Boston Herald American,
Sunday, December 3, 1978, A.M. Section D., 1.
Also interviewed by Time, Newsweek and the Washington
Post re: the booklet with Irvin Doress. CBS also
interested.

1979*

Professional Articles

"The Jewish Intellectual," Midstream, Vol. XXV, No. 1,
January 1979, 18-25.
"Some Social-Psychological Aspects of the Holocaust" in
Byron Sherwin (ed.) Encountering the Holocaust,
New York: Hebrew Publishing Company, 1979,
117-139.
"Sexuality and Judaism," Reconstructionist, February
1979. Vol. 44, No. 10.

---

*The second issue (Vol. 1, No. 2) of the Journal of the
History of Sociology came out in the Spring 1979.

"Kids in Cults" (with Irvin Doress) reprinted in Thomas
Robbins and Dick Anthony, In Gods We Trust: New
Patterns of Religious Pluralism, Transaction Books,
1979.

Essays

"Confronting the Media: The Impact of Jonestown on One
Sociologist," The New England Sociologist,
Spring-Summer 1979, Vol. 1, No. 2, 84-88.
"On Therapy, Research, and Other Dangerous Phenomena, "
Shoah: A Review of Holocaust Studies and
Commemorations, Vol. 1, No. 3, Winter 1979.
"Kids in Cults: Some Legal and Political Problems"
(with Irvin Doress), Sociological Abstracts (SSSP
Supplement No. 94), August 1979, 545.
"Tzedakah, Not Charity," Genesis 2, November 1979, 4.

Book Reviews

World of Our Fathers by Irving Howe in the American
Journal of Sociology, March 1979, Vol. 84, No. 5,
1310-1312.
Propaganda: The Second World War by Anthony Rhodes in
Qualitative Sociology, 1979.
Social Systems and the Evolution of Action Theory and
Action Theory and the Human Condition, both by
Talcott Parsons in the Journal of the History of
Sociology, Vol. 1, No. 2, Spring 1979, 114-117.
On the Margins of Science: The Social Construction of
Rejected Knowledge, ed. by Roy Wallis, in The
Humanist, Summer 1979.
Busing by Thomas J. Cottle in Women's American ORT
Reporter, November-December 1979, 19.

1980*

Professional Articles

"Martin Buber and the American Jewish Counterculture"
(with Yitzhak Ahren), Judaism: A Quarterly Journal,
#115, Vol. 29, No. 3, Summer 1980, 332-339.

---

*The third issue (Vol. 2, No. 1) of the Journal of the
history of Sociology. (special issue on Robert
Lynd) came out.

"Rosa Sonneschein and The American Jewess Revisited:
New Historical Information on an Early American
Zionist and Jewish Feminist", American Jewish
Archives, Vol. XXXII, No. 2, Nov. 1980, 125-131.

Essays

"The Origins of the Jewish Student Movement: A
Personal Reflection" in Genesis 2, 10th Anniversary
issue. Vol. II, No. 5, Feb. 1980, 19.

"The Affirmation of Life After the Holocaust: The
Contributions of Bettelheim, Lifton, and Frankl",
Association for Humanistic Psychology Newsletter,
August-September, 1980, 9-11.

"The Dilemma of the Yordim" in Dialogue: A Journal of
Jewish Voices, Summer 1980, 16-17.

"The Ten Commandments of the Holocaust", Jewish
Combatants of WW II: An Independent Illustrated
Quarterly Magazine, Vol. 1, No. 2, Fall, 1980.

Book Reviews

Palestinians Without Palestine by Alice and Yasumasa
Kuroda and Palestinian Society and Politics in
Contemporary Sociology, by Joel Migdal, Vol. 9,
1980.

Several book reviews on the history of sociology and
cognate fields, Journal of the History of
Sociology, Vol. 2, No. 2, Spring 1980.

Books

Second edition of The Sociology of American Jews
(University Press of America) came out in 1980.

Edited Vol. 2, No. 2 Spring 1980 issue of the Journal
of the History of Sociology.

Notes of a Happy Sociologist, Boston: Zalonka
Publications, June 1980.

Third and Fourth printing of Kids in Cults (with Irvin
Doress) 1980.

Review of the Journal of the History of Sociology in
Contemporary Sociology, Vol. 9, No. 2 March 1980,
p. 263-64. Fairly good. Reviewed by J. David Lewis
of University of Notre Dame.

The fourth issue (Vol. 2, No. 2), two full years, of
the Journal of the History of Sociology came out in
the late spring of 1980.

First issue, Vol. 1, No. 1, of the AAAE Newsletter,

Oct. 1980.
First issue, Vol. 1, No. 1, of the Sociology of
Business Newsletter, Nov. 1980.

1981

Professional Articles

"The Urban Middleman", Comparative Social Research,
Vol. 4, Summer 1981.
Various Entries in the Encyclopedia Judaica,
Supplementary Volume, ("Neo-Nazism", "Magnus
Hirschfeld", "Rosa Sonneschein"). (Came out in
1982).
"It Cann't Happen Here" (The Rise of Neo-Nazism in the
USA and Europe), Harvard Political Review, Vol. 8,
No. 3, Spring 1981, 12-14.
"What is Genocide?", Humanity and Sociology, Vol. 5,
No. 1, March 1981, 48-74.
"Is There a Survivor's Syndrome?", Journal of
Psychology and Judaism, Vol. 6, No. 1., Fall/Winter
1981, 33-52.

Essays

Symposium on the Institute for Policy Studies,
Midstream, February 1981, 44-45.
"Jewish Women in the Resistance" and Shmuel Parsov's
"Partisan Tales", Reprinted in Jewish Combatants of
World War II, Winter 1981, 24-30.

Book Reviews

Revolutionary Jews from Marx to Trotsky and Israel:
Utopia Inc. in the Journal of Ethnic Studies, Vol.
9, No. 3, Fall, 1981, 111-114.

Books, Monographs, etc.

The Jew as Outsider: Historical and Contemporary
Perspectives, University Press of America, 1981.
Jewish Partisans: A Documentary of Jewish Resistance
in the Soviet Union During WW II (Vol. 1) and
Jewish Partisans: Jewish Resistance in Europe
during WW II (Vol. 2), University Press of America
(Scheduled for 1981; appeared in 1982).
Genocide and Human Rights: A Global Anthology,
University Press of America (appeared in 1982).
Jews and the Cults: A Bibliography, Fresh Meadows, New

York: Biblio Press, 1981.
Volume 3, No. 1, of the Journal of the History of
Sociology appeared.
Volume 1, No. 2, of the Sociology of Business
Newsletter appeared.

1982

Professional Articles

"Radical Sociology Textbooks," Humboldt Journal of
Social Relations, Vol. 9, No. 1, Fall-Winter,
1981-82, 198-206.
"On Self-Hatred"; "Towards a Theory of Middlemen":
"The Image of Sociology in the Media"; and
"Science and Pseudo-Science", all in progress.
"Corporations that Grant Degrees," Business and Society
Review, No. 41, Spring 1982, 41-450.

Essays

Selections from Jewish Partisans, in Jewish Currents,
April, 1982.
"Notes of an Insider/Outsider," Judaica Book News, Vol.
12, No. 2,
"The Death of a Father," International Jewish Monthly,
(forthcoming),
"Dinner Speech," In honor of Morris U. Schappes,
Jewish Currents, (forthcoming).

Book Reviews

Quality of Working Life and the Kibbutz Experience by
Albert Cherns in Contemporary Sociology, Vol. 11,
No. 2, March 1982, 211.
Beyond Conflict: Black-Jewish Relations by Joyce Gelb
in The Journal of Ethnic Studies, Vol. 10, No. 1,
Spring 1982, 111-113.
Jewish Origins of the Psychoanalytic Movement by Dennis
Klein in Journal of the History of Behaviorial
Sciences, Vol. XVIII, No. 2, April 1982, 193-194.
America and the Survivors of the Holocaust, by Leonard
Dinnerstein in Judaica Book News, Fall 1982, forth-
coming.

Books, Monographs, Anthologies

Conflict and Conflict Resolution: An Historical
Bibliography, New York, Garland Press, 1982.

Handbook on Cults, Sects and Alternative Religions,
    Boston, Mass., Zalonka Publications, April 1982.
Confronting History and Holocaust: Collected Essays,
    Volume 2, Lanham, Maryland: University Press of
    America, (forthcoming).

SPEECHES AND LECTURES, 1971-1982

1) "Political Student Movements," Midwest Sociological Society, Minnepolis, May 1971.
2) "Language and Race: the Relationship between Blacks and Jews in America," Society for the Study of Social Problems, Denver, Colorado August 1971.
3) "Jewish Radicals," B'Nai Brith Anti-Defamation League Annual Convention, Grossinger's, New York, Nov. 21-24, 1971.
4) "Jewish Radicalism," (with Peter Dreier), American Sociological Association, New York, August 1973.
5) "Jewish Studies," panel-Society for the Study of Social Problems, New York, August 1973.
6) "Socialization into Sex Roles," North American Jewish Student Network Conference, Liberty, NY Dec. 23-25, 1973.
7) "The Role of the Jewish Intellectual in America," American Jewish Historical Society, Bi-centennial Series, Brandeis University, Jan. 8, 1976.
8) "Survival in Graduate School," American Sociological Association Professional Workshop, moderated by Emilio C. Viano, August 1976. (ASA annual meetings, New York City).
9) "Zionism, Racism, and the United Nations: Towards the Banalization of Language," Luncheon Roundtable Discussion, American Sociological Association Annual Meeting, organized by Carol Brown, New York City, August 1976.
10) "Victimization of the Victim," Second International Sympsium on Victomology, Chairman-Roger Hood of Oxford, Northeastern University, Boston, Wednesday, September 8, 1976, and
11) "The Political Criminal as Victim," Second International Symposium on Victomology, Chairman-Preben Wolf of Denmark, Friday, September 10, 1976.
12) "The Jewish Student Movement: Its Successes and Failures," American Jewish Historical Society, Lecture Series in honor of Louis Ruchames, Boston, Series Organizer, 1976.
13) Session Organizer -- "Genocide: A Global Perspective" -- 1977 American Sociological Association, September 1977, Chicago, Illinois.
14) "What is Genocide?", 1977 ASA meetings in Chicago, Illinois.

15) "The Art of Teaching," Massachusetts Sociological Association meetings, June 1977 (Mt. Holyoke College); Session: "Role Models in Teaching," June 10-11, 1977.

16) "The Nazis of America," Zionist House, Boston, January 10, 1978.

17) "Religion and Political Change: The Case of Jewish Radicalism," conducted seminar, Harvard University Divinity School, April 1978.

18) "Editing Historical Journals" (with Glenn Jacobs), 10th Annual Meeting of CHEIRON: The International Society for the History of the Behavioral and Social Sciences, Wellesley College, Friday, June 2, 1978.

19) "Do the Nazis Have the Right to March in Skokie?" Harvard Law School, March 10, 1978.

20) "On Teaching the Holocaust," Harvard School of Education, November 1978.

21) "Jewish Participation in the Partisan Movement," Association for the Sociological Study of Jewry, Sunday, August 26, 1979, Session: The Sociological Study of the Holocaust; Charles Glock -- discussant.

22) "What is Genocide?" the Third International Symposium on Victimology, University of Westphalia, Muenster, West Germany, September 4-8, 1979.

23) "Kids in Cults: Some Political and Legal Problems" (with Irvin Doress), Society for the Study of Social Problems, August 27, 1979), Boston.

24) Discussant for "The New Anti-Semitism," Society for the Study of Social Problems, Boston, August 27, 1979.

25) "Resistance to Genocide During World War II, with Comparisons to the Iranian Situation," Boston University, Iranian Student Association, June 15, 1979.

26) "On Self-Hatred; or was Karl Marx an Anti-Semite?", paper presented at the Eastern Sociological Association meetings, Boston, March 21-23, 1980, at the sociology of knowledge session.

27) Organizer and Presider of the session on "The Sociology of Jews", Eastern Sociological Association, March 21-23, 1980, Boston, Massachusetts.

28) "Black, Jews, and the Middle East: The Andrew Young Affair", paper presented at roundtable sessions, Eastern Sociological Society meetings, Boston, Massachusetts, March 21-23, 1980.

29) Testimony at White House Conference on Families,
    Hartford, Connecticut, February 26, 1980.
    Discussed the impact of religious cults on family.
30) Testimony in Boston, Gardner Auditorium, State
    House, June 3, 1980 on the need and focus of a
    National Academy of Peace and Conflict Resolution
    to the US Commission for such an academy.
31) "The Upsurge of Neo-Nazism in Europe and the USA",
    Harvard University, Center for European Studies,
    November 18, 1980.
32) "The Rise of Neo-Nazism Today, The Community Church
    of Boston, November 7, 1980.
33) "Jewish Family Camps in the Ukraine", Ukrainian
    Research Institute, Harvard University, December
    10, 1980.
34) "Neo-Nazi, Neo-Fascism, and Terrorism", Eastern
    Sociological Society, New York City, March 21-23,
    1981.
35) "Terrorism and Neo-Fascist Groups", Massachusetts
    Sociological Society, Regis College, 4-25-81.
36) "Religion, Cults, and the First Amendment", ACLU
    Conference, Boston College, 5-31-81.
37) "Toward a History of Conflict", Second
    International Organizational Development
    Conference, Nashua, New Hampshire, October 13,
    1981.
38) "Rescue and Responsibility During the Holocaust",
    Conference sponsored by Jewish Community Relations
    Council, South New Jersey, October 16, 1981.
39) Keynote speaker, Armenian Book Festival,
    Providence, Rhode Island, October 25, 1981.
40) Invited to present paper on genocide at the First
    International Conference on the Holocaust and
    Genocide, Jerusalem, Israel, June 20-24, 1982.
    (could not attend).
41) "What is Genocide?--A Legal Perspectative",
    University of Bridgeport, School of Law, February
    16, 1982, Bridgeport, Connecticut.
42) Christian-Jewish Dialogue on the Holocaust, Gordon
    College, Wenham, Massachusetts, March 13, 1982.
43) The Jewish Rebel: Radicals, Feminists,
    Progressives in History", Jewish Feminists
    Conference, Harvard University Hillel, March 28,
    1982.
44) "The Children of Holocaust Survivors", Boston
    Psychoanalytic Society, Monday, April 12, 1982.
45) "Neo-Nazism, Neo-Fascism, and Terrorism",
    Massachusetts Sociological Society, Boston State
    College, Saturday, April 24, 1982.

46) "Coercive Methods in Cults", Testimony before the New York State Assembly, New York City, May 13, 1982.

47) Testimonial Remarks in honor of Morris Schappes Dinner, New York City, Sunday, May 2, 1982.

48) "The Jewish Rebel", BBN--Jewish Community Center, Boston, April 1, 1982.

49) "Nazis Collaborators in the USA", Various lectures in Boston, May, 1982.

50) "Science and Pseudo-Science", Various lectures in Boston, May, 1982.

IV. ABOUT THE AUTHOR

ABOUT THE AUTHOR

JACK NUSAN PORTER is a sociologist, author, editor, and political activist. Born in Ukraine and raised in Milwaukee, he graduated cum laude from the University of Wisconsin-Milwaukee and received his Ph.D. in sociology from Northwestern University in 1971.

He has published fifteen books and anthologies and nearly 150 articles, including Student Protest and the Technocratic Society, The Study of Society (contributing editor), Jewish Radicalism (with Peter Dreier), The Sociology of American Jews, The Jew as Outsider: Collected Essays, Kids in Cults (with Irvin Doress), Conflict and Conflict Resolution, Jewish Partisans (two volumes), and Genocide and Human Rights. He has made many contributions to reference books and journals including the Encyclopedia Judaica, Encyclopedia of Sociology, Society, Midstream, and Writer's Digest.

He is the founder of the Journal of the History of Sociology and the Sociology of Business Newsletter and the winner of the John Atherton Fellowship from the Breadloaf Writers' Conference as well as fellowships from the Memorial Foundation for Jewish Culture and the World Jewish Congress. He is listed in Who's Who in the East, American Men and Women of Science, Who's Who in Israel, and Contemporary Authors.

Dr. Porter has lectured widely on American social problems and political/religious movements. He has testified before several government commissions including the White House Conference on Families and the National Peace Academy hearings. Long active in Israel and Jewish communal activities, he is considered one of the founders of the Jewish student movement in the USA and Canada in the late 1960's.

He lives with his wife Miriam, their son Gabriel and daughter Danielle in Boston, where he is a research associate at Harvard University at the Ukrainian Research Institute.

RIGHTS AND PERMISSIONS